Macroeconomics for MBAs and Masters of Finance

Morris A. Davis

CAMBRIDGE
UNIVERSITY PRESS

CAMBRIDGE UNIVERSITY PRESS
Cambridge, New York, Melbourne, Madrid, Cape Town,
Singapore, São Paulo, Delhi, Tokyo, Mexico City

Cambridge University Press
The Edinburgh Building, Cambridge CB2 8RU, UK

Published in the United States of America by
Cambridge University Press, New York

www.cambridge.org
Information on this title: www.cambridge.org/9780521762472

First published 2009
Reprinted 2011

A catalogue record for this publication is available from the British Library

Library of Congress Cataloguing in Publication data
Davis, Morris A., 1972–
Macroeconomics for MBAs and masters of finance / Morris A. Davis.
    p.   cm.
Includes bibliographical references and index.
ISBN 978-0-521-76247-2 (hardback)
1. Macroeconomics.   I. Title.
HB172.5.D378   2009
339 – dc22   2009038166

ISBN 978-0-521-76247-2 Hardback

Contents

List of Figures	*page*	ix
List of Tables		xii
Preface		xv
Foreword		xix

1	**GDP and Inflation**	1
	Objectives of this Chapter	2
1.1	GDP	3
	1.1.1 Definition of GDP	3
	1.1.2 GDP and Welfare	9
	1.1.3 Historical Behavior of Nominal and Real GDP	11
	1.1.4 Caveats	15
1.2	Components of GDP	15
	1.2.1 Private Consumption	16
	1.2.2 Private Investment	20
	1.2.3 Government Spending	22
	1.2.4 Net Exports	25
	1.2.5 Miscellany	27
1.3	More GDP Accounting	28
1.4	Inflation	31
	Further Reading	37
	Homework	38

2	**Firms and Growth**	43
	Objectives of this Chapter	44
2.1	Cobb–Douglas Production	45

	2.1.1 Constant Returns to Scale	46
	2.1.2 Declining Marginal Products	47
2.2	Profit Maximization	48
	2.2.1 Optimal Capital	49
	2.2.2 Optimal Labor	51
	2.2.3 Optimal Profits	51
2.3	Growth Accounting	52
	2.3.1 Growth in Developed Countries	55
	2.3.2 Balanced Growth	56
	2.3.3 Growth in Developing Countries	58
	2.3.4 Barriers to Growth	60
2.4	Measurement of K_t, L_t, and z_t	68
	2.4.1 Measurement of the Capital Stock	68
	2.4.2 Measurement of the Labor Input	76
	2.4.3 Measurement of Technology	80
	Further Reading	83
	Homework	84
3	**Households and Asset Pricing**	**89**
	Objectives of this Chapter	90
3.1	Optimal Labor Supply with No Saving	93
3.2	Optimal Consumption and Investment	97
	3.2.1 A Two-Period Model	97
	3.2.2 Mathematics of the Solution	99
	3.2.3 Reinterpreting the Household Budget Constraint	101
	3.2.4 Intertemporal Elasticity of Substitution	102
	3.2.5 Discussion of Assumptions	104
	3.2.6 Discussion of Uncertainty	106
3.3	Saving and Investment in Multiple Assets	109
	3.3.1 Stocks and Bonds: The Equity Premium Puzzle	109
	3.3.2 Housing	118

3.4   Optimal Labor, Consumption, Investment   129
       3.4.1 Model   129
       3.4.2 Calibration   133
       Further Reading   134
       Homework   136

4   **Trade**   141
       Objectives of this Chapter   142
4.1   Trade of Goods for Goods   144
4.2   Current and Capital Accounts   148
4.3   Data on Current and Capital Accounts   150
4.4   Trade of Goods for Assets   152
4.5   Factor Prices and Trade   159
4.6   Topics in Exchange Rates   161
       4.6.1 Covered Interest Parity   161
       4.6.2 Purchasing Power Parity   162
       4.6.3 Fisher Equation   163
       Further Reading   164
       Homework   165

5   **Business Cycles**   167
       Objectives of this Chapter   168
5.1   Business Cycle Dates   169
5.2   Trends and Cycles   169
5.3   Business Cycle Statistics   178
5.4   The Theory of Business Cycles   184
       Further Reading   186
       Homework   189

6 Monetary Policy   191
   Objectives of this Chapter   192
6.1 A Very Brief History of the Federal Reserve   192
6.2 The Taylor Rule   196
6.3 Monetary Policy and Inflation   201
   Further Reading   205
   Homework   207

Appendix: Math   209
   Objectives of this Appendix   209
A.1 Derivatives   209
   A.1.1 Derivative of Polynomials   210
   A.1.2 Derivative of the Natural Logarithm Function   212
   A.1.3 Derivative Approximation to the Natural
         Logarithm Function   213
A.2 Constrained Optimization: Econ 1 Revealed   214
   A.2.1 Writing Down and Solving the Problem   215
   A.2.2 Notes on the Lagrange Multiplier (λ) and
         Expenditure Shares   217

   Bibliography   219
   Index   223

Figures

1.1 Annual log real GDP and "trend" log real GDP,
   1929–2007   *page* 13
1.2 Annual log real GDP and trend log real GDP,
   1973–2007   14
1.3 Annual log real GDP and log nominal GDP,
   1929–2007   14
1.4 Ratio of annual nominal consumption (excluding
   durables) to annual nominal GDP, 1929–2007   18
1.5 Detrended log real consumption (excluding durables)
   and log real GDP, 1929–2007   19
1.6 Detrended log real consumption (excluding durables)
   and log real GDP, 1973–2007   19
1.7 Ratio of annual nominal gross private domestic
   investment to annual nominal GDP, 1929–2007   21
1.8 Detrended log real gross private domestic investment
   and detrended log real GDP, 1973–2007   22
1.9 Bureau of Economic Analysis National Income and
   Product Accounts Table 1.10: Gross domestic income
   by type of income   29
1.10 Capital's share of income (α), 1929–2007   31
1.11 Annual inflation rate, all consumption and
   consumption excl. food and energy, 1930–2007   33
1.12 Annual inflation rate, all consumption and
   consumption excl. food and energy, 1997–2007   34
1.13 Annual inflation rate, investment in equipment and
   software, 1930–2007   35

1.14 Annual inflation rate, owner-occupied housing
(from www.ofheo.gov), 1975–2007   36
2.1   Bureau of Economic Analysis Fixed Asset Table 1.1:
Current-cost net stock of fixed assets and consumer
durable goods   70
2.2   Bureau of Economic Analysis National Income and
Product Accounts Table 1.1.5: Gross domestic product   71
2.3   Bureau of Economic Analysis National Income and
Product Accounts Table 2.3.5: Personal consumption
expenditures by major type of product   72
2.4   The ratio of the nominal value of capital to nominal
annual output, 1929–2006   73
2.5   The depreciation rate of capital, δ, 1930–2006   74
2.6   Per-capita hours worked per week, 1949–2006   78
2.7 $\ln(z_t)$ and its trend, with $\ln(z_t)$ rescaled to 0.0 in
1949, 1949–2006   81
2.8   Deviations of $\ln(z_t)$ from trend, 1949–2006   82
3.1   Realized values of ϵ_{t+1}, 1949–2007   115
3.2   Ratio of annual rents to house prices (percent),
1960:1–2007:4   127
3.3   Nominal interest rate on 10-year Treasury Bonds,
1995–2007   128
4.1   Net exports, exports, and imports as a percentage of
nominal GDP, 1929–2007   151
5.1   Quarterly change in log real GDP and dates of NBER
contractions, 1949:1–2007:4   170
5.2   Log real GDP, 1949:1–2007:4   172
5.3   Trend log real GDP, trend computed using the
HP-Filter and a straight line, 1949:1–2007:4   173
5.4   Log real GDP less trend, trend computed using the
HP-Filter and a straight line, 1949:1–2007:4   174

5.5   Detrended real GDP and detrended real consumption
excl. durables, 1949:1–2007:4   179

5.6   Detrended real GDP and detrended real investment,
1949:1–2007:4   179

5.7   Detrended real GDP and detrended hours worked,
1949:1–2007:3   180

6.1   Nominal federal Funds Rate and predicted nominal
Federal Funds Rate using equation (6.2),
1987:1–2007:4   200

6.2   Trend $g_M - g_Y$ and trend g_P, annual rates,
1959:1–2007:4   204

6.3   Trend g_M and trend g_P, annual rates, 1959:1–2007:4   205

A.1   Graph of $f(x) = -5(x-3)^2$, with tangent lines at
$x = 0$ and $x = 3$ 210

A.2   Graph of $3 \ln(x)$ 212

Tables

1.1	Simple GDP example	*page* 7
1.2	Annual nominal government expenditures in 2007	23
2.1	Real per-capita (PC) GDP (constant US$2000) in 1973 and 2003, and growth in real PC GDP 1973–2003, 10 poorest and 10 richest countries as of 1973*	61
2.2	Real per-capita (PC) GDP (constant US$2000) in 1973 and 2003, and growth in real PC GDP 1973–2003, 10 poorest and 10 richest countries as of 2003	63
2.3	Effective tax rates (%), 1996, G7 countries	75
3.1	Relationship of σ and risk aversion	117
3.2	Rent-price ratio by MSA, 2000	125
3.3	Comparison of rent-price ratio by MSA in 2000 with growth in house prices from 2000 to 2007	126
4.1	Bjørn and François production possibilities	144
4.2	Bjørn and François production: autarky	145
4.3	Bjørn and François production with some specialization	145
4.4	Bjørn and François production and consumption after some specialization	146
4.5	US exports and imports of goods in $ millions in 2007 by major region	152
4.6	North and South production possibilities of tons of food	153
4.7	North and South production and consumption after trade	154
4.8	Bjørn and François production: autarky	156
4.9	Bjørn and François production: some specialization	156

4.10 Bjørn and François production and consumption after
     some specialization   156
5.1 NBER business cycle dates   170
5.2 Percentage standard deviations   182
5.3 Correlations   183
6.1 Chairmen of the Federal Reserve Board   194

Preface

In June 2006, the Dean here at Wisconsin School of Business at the University of Wisconsin-Madison, Mike Knetter, asked me to teach a five-week segment on macroeconomics to the first-year full-time MBA students. After some thought, I decided on three goals for the course.

First, I wanted to teach what I considered to be the essential components of modern macroeconomics. This includes, at a minimum: the theory of firms and long-term growth implications; the theory of households and asset-pricing implications; the availability and history of the macroeconomic data on which these theories are based and tested; and then, if time permitted, trade, business cycles, and monetary policy. I figured that if the MBAs were exposed to what I considered essential macroeconomics, they would not confuse daily changes in stock prices with true macroeconomic phenomena.

Second, I wanted to emphasize the ideas generally agreed upon by academic macroeconomists, for example the nature of aggregate production and growth. At the same time, I wanted to downplay or ignore areas of research that are hotly contested, such as the efficacy (or lack thereof) of monetary policy at stabilizing the business cycle.

Third, I wanted the course to be mathematically rigorous but accessible with some modest effort. There are a few reasons for the rigor. A bit of mathematics allows key ideas to be taught quickly and precisely. Also, students studying for a Masters degree should be held to a higher standard than students taking an undergraduate intro course. Finally, I wanted to show students how economists think about the world: economists study the logical outcomes arising from well-specified models of endowments, preferences, and technology.

This leads me to this book. When I was evaluating textbooks for the MBA class I was a bit disappointed with what I saw. To start, in general, the books are not rigorous enough. Many of the available macroeconomics textbooks are not demanding enough of a mid-twenties college graduate studying for an advanced business degree. Second, they aren't that useful: they don't show the students how to download and access the key data, what the data look like, and why. And third, the textbooks I saw tended to emphasize areas where there is a lot of debate in the profession, such as the cause of business cycles and the usefulness of monetary policy.

Finally, many textbooks were quite lengthy! The essentials of macroeconomics can be taught quickly, if some basic math is used. In this book, we cover firms and growth by working with a representative firm that produces according to a Cobb–Douglas production function, and we study household consumption and savings and the implied asset-pricing implications using a two-period model where a representative household has time-separable log preferences for consumption. In my mind, this is the simplest framework that gets at the essence of modern macroeconomics. To understand the mathematics of the book, the readers need to know how to take the derivatives of a polynomial (for Cobb–Douglas production) and the natural log function (for household utility). The mathematical appendix inelegantly reviews the key mathematics used in this book.

This book is organized as follows: In the first chapter I define key macroeconomic variables such as GDP and inflation, and also document where the key macroeconomic data are located and their historical patterns. In the second chapter, I cover firm behavior which naturally leads to the theory of growth. In the third chapter, I cover household behavior (specifically consumption, saving, and labor supply decisions) which naturally leads to a theory of asset pricing.

The fourth, fifth, and sixth chapters are short chapters that cover important topics in macroeconomics, but in much less detail. The fourth chapter is a stand-alone chapter on trade. Using the simple idea of comparative advantage, I cover the topics of intratemporal trade (goods for goods) and intertemporal trade (goods for assets). I also cover the impact of trade on domestic interest rates and wage rates, and the topics of covered interest parity, purchasing power parity, and the Fisher equation. The fifth chapter covers business cycles and the sixth chapter covers monetary policy. These chapters focus more on the data, and are more loose in the theory, in the following sense: I do not really explain why business cycles occur because I myself am unsure,[1] and I do not explain the theory of why US policymakers adjust or do not adjust the Federal Funds Rate, which is the overnight rate at which banks borrow reserves.

At the end of each chapter I include a "Further Reading" section, which lists a few potentially interesting and related topics that I do not cover. In some of these cases, I direct the students to entries of the website Wikipedia. I understand there can be prejudice against Wikipedia, sometimes with good reason, but in the specific cases I reference I believe the Wikipedia entries are as informative as more conventional sources. Wikipedia has the added benefit that it is quickly available by anyone with web access. I should note that all the websites cited in the book were accessed and found to be accurate in May 2009.

For my five-week MBA class, I cover (in this order) Chapters 1 and 2 and the first half of Chapter 3 up through the equity-premium puzzle.[2] Sometimes we can cover some material from Chapters 4–6, but most times not. For my evening and executive MBA classes, which have fewer hours, I cover the chapter on trade and then the

---

[1] In my own research, business cycles are the result of "shocks" to the level of technology.

[2] I introduce mathematics from the appendix as the need arises.

less-technical material in Chapters 1 and 2. For a full-semester class of full-time MBAs or Masters students in finance, I would simply teach the book in order.

Before I conclude, I want to explain the cover. The cover is meant to look like a Ramones album. To me, the Ramones represent rock's reaction to progressive rock. Prog rock ("prog") songs are typically long and boring with lots of embellishment and orchestration. Ramones tunes are short, straight, and to the point – no monkey business! I would like to believe that this book is to current macro textbooks what the Ramones are to prog.

I owe a great deal of thanks to many people. First, I thank my colleagues here at the business school at the University of Wisconsin-Madison who suffered through early drafts of this book and contributed intellectually to its contents. Specifically, I owe quite a bit to Don Hausch (who co-teaches the economics course to our full-time MBAs with me), Mike Knetter, and my colleagues in the Real Estate department: François Ortalo-Magné, Stephen Malpezzi, and Tim Riddiough. Second, I thank Chris Harrison at Cambridge University Press, who has been both patient and generous with his time. Neither he nor any of his colleagues at Cambridge University Press have tried to appreciably alter the tone and/or contents of this book. Finally, I thank my wife Kim, and kids Jackson, Lauren, and Brett. They haven't done so much for this book, but they put up with a lot.

Foreword

Perhaps it's not immediately obvious why an applied microeconomist would write a preface for a macroeconomics text. Some might even say that it's not such a good idea. Nevertheless, I am pleased to introduce you to Morris Davis's *Macroeconomics for MBAs and Masters of Finance*.

Years ago, the first course I ever taught was, in fact, introductory macroeconomics. I thought then, and still do, that it would be great to have a concise introduction that was somehow both practical and rigorous. Finally, we have that book, and you're holding it in your hand.

Morris Davis is on the faculty of the Department of Real Estate and Urban Land Economics in the Wisconsin School of Business, where he's also a fellow of the James A. Graaskamp Center for Real Estate. After a strong training in economics at the University of Pennsylvania, Morris was an economist at the Board of Governors of the Federal Reserve before we persuaded him to move to Madison.

Our Dean, Michael Knetter, is himself a macro and trade economist of some repute. When we hired Morris a few years ago, Mike noticed Morris's strong training and practical experience in macroeconomics. The Dean proposed that in addition to real estate, we assign him to teach our core macro course to MBAs. Professor Davis readily agreed. Unable to find a concise, rigorous yet practical textbook when I taught macro many years ago, I whined and then made do with what I could find. Morris took direct action, and over the summer before his first semester's teaching wrote one!

It's an impressive little book. In a little over 200 pages Morris covers the basics of national income accounting, firms and growth, households and asset pricing, business cycles, trade, and just a touch of monetary theory and policy. And you get an appendix with that. For a number of MBAs, finally understanding how constrained optimization works (since most intro calculus courses ignore it, but it's the mathematical underpinning of most economics) is alone worth the price of admission.

The book has been field-tested by several cohorts of Wisconsin MBAs, and is ready to burst onto a bigger stage. I'm especially a fan of Chapter 1, since I'm an empiricist and I think every business man and woman needs to know how we measure the economy. Most of us know far too little. But data need a framework to really be useful, and the rest of the book will teach you how economists think about aggregate economies.

You have a hint about some of Professor Davis's interests beyond economics from the front cover. Morris is known not only for his excellent teaching and path-breaking research but also for the solid groove he sets down as bassist for The Contractions, probably – no, certainly – the best rock band ever comprised completely of economists. MP3s and more at http://contractions.marginalq.com/. Move some to your iPod for the perfect soundtrack to accompany your study of the aggregate economy.

Enjoy!

Steve Malpezzi
Madison, Wisconsin

1 | GDP and Inflation

O Objectives of this Chapter

We start this chapter by defining gross domestic product, GDP. GDP is the most useful and important summary statistic describing aggregate domestic production. We explain the conceptual difference between nominal and real GDP and then document the historical behavior of both the nominal and real GDP data. We explain how the growth rate of real GDP is computed and then explain why, under certain conditions, growth in real GDP reflects aggregate changes to well-being.

Next, we show that GDP can be viewed as the sum of four components relating to spending by households, firms, and the government. These four components are consumption, investment, government, and net exports. The description of GDP as the sum of these four components is commonly called the "the expenditure method" for computing GDP. We explain why disaggregating GDP into these particular components is useful, and discuss specific patterns in the historical data related to each component.

Next, we note that the rules of accounting imply that aggregate expenditures equal aggregate income. For this reason, GDP can also be measured as the sum of income accruing to all sources. This method of computing GDP is commonly referred to as the "income method." We divide aggregate income earned by all sources into income earned by capital and income earned by labor. We show that the shares of aggregate income earned by capital and labor have been roughly constant over history.

In the final part of the chapter, we define inflation – the rate of change of the price level – and show the historical data on consumer-price inflation in the United States.

1.1 GDP

1.1.1 Definition of GDP

The key difference between microeconomics and macroeconomics is that microeconomists tend to study one market at a time and in isolation, whereas macroeconomists study the interaction of all markets together.

The study of the interaction of all markets sounds like an impossibly complex project. How can we describe the interaction of the production of apples, bananas, computers, cars, airplanes, frozen orange juice, financial services, etc. in one book?

One possibility is to study, in great detail, each market separately and then try to make sense of it all. Macroeconomists employ a different tactic: they add up all of the output that is produced in all of the sectors of the economy (apples, bananas, computers, etc.) and study the sum. This sum is called GDP which stands for "gross domestic product." Nominal GDP is the dollar value of all output – goods and services – produced in the United States. Real GDP is something else: conceptually, real GDP measures the quantity of all goods and services that are produced.

Let's use a simple example to make these ideas concrete. Suppose everyone in the United States picks apples from trees. Denote the price of apples in US\$ in the year 2000 as $p_{a,2000}$ and the number of apples picked in 2000 as a_{2000}. Nominal GDP in US\$ in 2000 would equal $p_{a,2000} * a_{2000}$ (the price of apples times the number of apples picked), and real GDP would equal a_{2000}, the number of apples picked. Growth in nominal GDP between 2000 and 2001 would be

$$\frac{p_{a,2001} * a_{2001}}{p_{a,2000} * a_{2000}},$$

and growth in real GDP would be

$$\frac{a_{2001}}{a_{2000}}.$$

In this simple example, growth in nominal GDP is equal to growth in real GDP multiplied by growth in apple prices. Real GDP increases when more apples are picked. Nominal GDP increases more rapidly than real GDP when the price of apples increases.

Suppose that the only argument in the utility function of households in the United States is the quantity of apples. In this case, positive growth of real GDP tells us that standards of living have increased: there are more apples and thus more utility. Growth in nominal GDP is less informative about changes to standards of living. If nominal GDP increases because apple prices have increased, but the production of apples has not changed, then household utility is unchanged. Thus, a key idea in this chapter is that growth in real GDP, and not nominal GDP, is informative about changes to aggregate production.

It gets tricky to think about the relevance or even the measurement of something called GDP if more than one good is produced in the economy. Suppose that everyone in the United States picks either apples or bananas from trees. Denoting the price of bananas in US$ in 2000 as $p_{b,2000}$ and the quantity picked of bananas in 2000 as b_{2000}, nominal GDP in US$ in 2000 would equal $p_{a,2000} * a_{2000} + p_{b,2000} * b_{2000}$: this is the sum of the value of all apples picked and all bananas picked. In this sense, nominal GDP is quite easy to measure: just add up the dollar value of everything that is produced![1]

But how would we go about defining and measuring real GDP such that changes to real GDP are informative of changes to aggregate production? For example, suppose 5 apples and 10 bananas are picked in 2000 and 4 apples and 11 bananas are picked in 2001. More bananas

---

[1] Although measuring nominal GDP seems easy, in practice it requires the full-time work of a staff of many economists.

are picked in 2001 than in 2000, but fewer apples. Has aggregate production increased or decreased?

Here is an accurate approximation of the procedure that has been established. First, a base year (currently 2000) is arbitrarily chosen in which real GDP equals nominal GDP. Then, real GDP in 2001 is approximately[2] computed as the price of apples and bananas in 2000 times the quantity of apples and bananas picked in 2001:

$$p_{a,2000} * a_{2001} + p_{b,2000} * b_{2001}.$$

Given this definition, the percentage growth in real GDP in 2001 is computed as follows:[3]

$$\frac{\text{real } GDP_{2001}}{\text{real } GDP_{2000}} - 1.0 = \frac{p_{a,2000} * a_{2001} + p_{b,2000} * b_{2001}}{p_{a,2000} * a_{2000} + p_{b,2000} * b_{2000}} - 1.0.$$

With some algebra, real GDP growth from 2000 to 2001 reduces to an interesting and convenient expression:

$$= \left(\frac{p_{a,2000} * a_{2001}}{p_{a,2000} * a_{2000} + p_{b,2000} * b_{2000}} \right)$$

$$+ \left(\frac{p_{b,2000} * b_{2001}}{p_{a,2000} * a_{2000} + p_{b,2000} * b_{2000}} \right) - 1.0$$

$$= \left(\frac{p_{a,2000} * a_{2000}}{p_{a,2000} * a_{2000} + p_{b,2000} * b_{2000}} \right) \left(\frac{a_{2001}}{a_{2000}} \right)$$

$$+ \left(\frac{p_{b,2000} * b_{2000}}{p_{a,2000} * a_{2000} + p_{b,2000} * b_{2000}} \right) \left(\frac{b_{2001}}{b_{2000}} \right) - 1.0$$

$$= \widehat{\phi}_{2000} \left(\frac{a_{2001}}{a_{2000}} \right) + \left(1 - \widehat{\phi}_{2000} \right) \left(\frac{b_{2001}}{b_{2000}} \right) - 1.0.$$

The second equation follows from the first because a_{2001} is identically equal to $a_{2000} * \frac{a_{2001}}{a_{2000}}$ (and b_{2000} has a similar expression). In the third

---

[2] The way real GDP growth between 2000 and 2001 is computed in this example is not completely accurate for technical reasons discussed later.

[3] For any two numbers x_1 and x_2, the percentage difference of x_1 and x_2 is $(x_2 - x_1)/x_1 = x_2/x_1 - 1.0$.

equation, we have defined the variable $\widehat{\phi}_{2000}$ as

$$\widehat{\phi}_{2000} = \frac{p_{a,2000} * a_{2000}}{p_{a,2000} * a_{2000} + p_{b,2000} * b_{2000}}.$$

$\widehat{\phi}_{2000}$ is the measured expenditure share on apples in 2000 – it is the fraction of nominal GDP attributable to the value of apples. Analogously, $1 - \widehat{\phi}_{2000}$ is the measured expenditure share on bananas in 2000.

In other words, we have shown that real GDP growth from 2000 to 2001 is equal to the measured expenditure share on apples in 2000 multiplied by the growth in the quantity of apples between 2000 and 2001 plus the measured expenditure share on bananas in 2000 multiplied by the growth in the quantity of bananas.

Real GDP growth from 2001 to 2002 is defined analogously:

$$\frac{\text{real } GDP_{2002}}{\text{real } GDP_{2001}} - 1.0$$

$$= \frac{p_{a,2001} * a_{2002} + p_{b,2001} * b_{2002}}{p_{a,2001} * a_{2001} + p_{b,2001} * b_{2001}} - 1.0$$

$$= \widehat{\phi}_{2001}\left(\frac{a_{2002}}{a_{2001}}\right) + \left(1 - \widehat{\phi}_{2001}\right)\left(\frac{b_{2002}}{b_{2001}}\right) - 1.0.$$

It is the measured expenditure share on apples in 2001 multiplied by the growth in the quantity of apples from 2001 to 2002 plus the measured expenditure share on bananas in 2001 multiplied by the growth in the quantity of bananas from 2001 to 2002.

It is important to emphasize that the level of real GDP is totally meaningless, since the base year for which nominal GDP and real GDP coincide is arbitrarily chosen. However, growth in real GDP does not depend on the base year baseline level of real GDP. One way to see this is to reconsider growth in real GDP between 2000 and 2001, but divide both the numerator and denominator of the mathematical

Table 1.1 Simple GDP example								
Year	a	p_a	b	p_b	$a * p_a$	$b * p_b$	Nom. GDP	Real GDP $2000 apple equiv.
								$2000
2000	5	$20.0	10	$15.0	$100.0	$150.0	$250.0	$250.0　12.50
2001	4	$25.0	11	$15.5	$100.0	$170.5	$270.5	$245.0　12.25

expression by the price of apples in 2000, $p_{a,2000}$:

$$\frac{\text{real } GDP_{2001}}{\text{real } GDP_{2000}} - 1.0 = \frac{p_{a,2000} * a_{2001} + p_{b,2000} * b_{2001}}{p_{a,2000} * a_{2000} + p_{b,2000} * b_{2000}} - 1.0$$

$$= \frac{a_{2001} + b_{2001} * \left(\frac{p_{b,2000}}{p_{a,2000}}\right)}{a_{2000} + b_{2000} * \left(\frac{p_{b,2000}}{p_{a,2000}}\right)} - 1.0.$$

The numerator and denominator of the expression above are equal to real GDP in 2001 and 2000, respectively, in units of apples at year-2000 prices (rather than real GDP in constant year-2000 dollars). The denominator represents the quantity of apples picked in 2000 assuming all bananas picked in 2000 are exchanged for apples at the market price for apples in 2000 (this is the $b_{2000} * \left(p_{b,2000}/p_{a,2000}\right)$ term). The numerator represents the quantity of apples picked in 2001 assuming that all bananas picked in year 2001 can be exchanged for apples at year-2000 relative prices for bananas and apples.

The simple example in Table 1.1 further highlights the irrelevance of the level of real GDP and the importance of growth in real GDP. Note the expenditure share on apples in 2000 in this table is 40 percent ($0.4 = \$100/\$250$) and the expenditure share on bananas is 60 percent. According to the expenditure share method, growth in real GDP between 2000 and 2001 is -2.0%:

$$0.4 * \left(\frac{4}{5}\right) + 0.6 * \left(\frac{11}{10}\right) - 1.0 = -0.02.$$

In terms of constant $2000, real GDP is $250.00 in 2000 and $245 in 2001. The $245 value for real GDP in 2001 reflects -2% real GDP growth between 2000 and 2001, i.e. $245 = 250 * (1.0 - 0.02)$.

If we were to compute real GDP in apple equivalents at year-2000 relative prices, we would compute real GDP to be 12.50 apple equivalents in the year 2000 and 12.25 apple equivalents in the year 2001:

$$\text{Year 2000:} \quad 12.50 = 5 + 10 * \left(\frac{\$15.00}{\$20.00} \right)$$

$$\text{Year 2001:} \quad 12.25 = 4 + 11 * \left(\frac{\$15.00}{\$20.00} \right).$$

Growth in real GDP when measured in apple equivalents is $12.25/12.50 - 1.0 = -0.02(-2.0\%)$, which is identical to growth in real GDP between 2000 and 2001 when GDP is measured in constant $2000. This example demonstrates that the growth rates of real GDP do not depend on whether the level of real GDP is measured in apple equivalents or in constant $2000.

There are a few more facts about real GDP of which you should be aware:

• In our examples, we updated the expenditure shares every year when calculating growth in real GDP. In other words, to compute real GDP growth from 2000 to 2001, we used year-2000 expenditure shares, and to compute real GDP growth from 2001 to 2002, we used year-2001 expenditure shares. If we had worked with quarterly examples, we would have updated expenditure shares every quarter. The period-by-period updating of expenditure shares is consistent with current practice at the government agency that constructs the GDP data, the Bureau of Economic Analysis (BEA).[4]

---

[4] Before 1996, the BEA held expenditure shares fixed at some base year, and the base year was updated every five years. This method led to large revisions in estimated

- As a technical aside, note that the BEA does not use previous-year expenditure shares to compute real rates of growth from period to period. Rather, the BEA averages expenditure shares from the current and previous periods in its computations. I have defined real GDP growth using previous-period expenditure shares so the link between GDP growth and welfare is exact, discussed later in this chapter.
- In earlier decades, macroeconomists studied GNP, "gross national product," which is the output of all citizens, not all of which is necessarily produced on US soil. In this book I focus on GDP, which has become the preferred measure.

1.1.2 GDP and Welfare

Growth in real GDP as we have calculated it provides a quick summary of the pace at which production of goods and services across the entire economy has been increasing. But does real GDP growth (the way we have measured it) inform us of changes to living standards? It turns out, under certain assumptions, that we can map changes to utility with changes to real GDP growth.

As you may have learned in your microeconomics class, the mathematical function that determines a ranking of household preferences over different combinations of goods is called as a utility function; and, in your previous classes, you may have seen many different kinds of utility functions. For our purposes, suppose households have time-invariant preferences – preferences that do not change over time – for apples and bananas that are described by the following utility function

$$\phi \ln(a) + (1 - \phi) \ln(b), \tag{1.1}$$

real rates of growth after base years were updated – expenditure shares on certain items (for example, computer software) have changed markedly over time.

with $0 < \phi < 1$. Given production of a_{2000} apples and b_{2000} bananas in 2000, utility in 2000 is

$$u_{2000} = \phi \ln (a_{2000}) + (1 - \phi) \ln (b_{2000}).$$

Likewise, utility in 2001 given a_{2001} apples and b_{2001} bananas produced in 2001 is

$$u_{2001} = \phi \ln (a_{2001}) + (1 - \phi) \ln (b_{2001}).$$

How does u_{2001} compare to u_{2000}? $u_{2001} - u_{2000}$ is equal to

$$[\phi \ln(a_{2001}) + (1 - \phi) \ln(b_{2001})] - [\phi \ln(a_{2000})$$
$$+ (1 - \phi) \ln(b_{2000})]$$
$$= \phi [\ln(a_{2001}) - \ln(a_{2000})] + (1 - \phi)[\ln(b_{2001})$$
$$- \ln(b_{2000})] \tag{1.2}$$

$$= \phi \ln \left(\frac{a_{2001}}{a_{2000}} \right) + (1 - \phi) \ln \left(\frac{b_{2001}}{b_{2000}} \right) \tag{1.3}$$

$$= \phi \ln \left(1 + \frac{a_{2001} - a_{2000}}{a_{2000}} \right)$$
$$+ (1 - \phi) \ln \left(1 + \frac{b_{2001} - b_{2000}}{b_{2000}} \right) \tag{1.4}$$

$$\approx \phi \left(\frac{a_{2001} - a_{2000}}{a_{2000}} \right) + (1 - \phi) \left(\frac{b_{2001} - b_{2000}}{b_{2000}} \right) \tag{1.5}$$

$$= \phi \left(\frac{a_{2001}}{a_{2000}} \right) + (1 - \phi) \left(\frac{b_{2001}}{b_{2000}} \right) - 1. \tag{1.6}$$

Equation (1.3) follows from equation (1.2) because of the properties of the natural logarithm;[5] equation (1.5) approximately follows[6]

---

[5] See the appendix for details.   [6] The $\approx$ sign means "approximately equal to."

from (1.4) because of the properties of the derivative of the natural logarithm.[7] Equation (1.6) follows from (1.5) from simple algebra.

In the appendix, we prove that when households have preferences for apples and bananas as given by equation (1.1), ϕ is the optimal household expenditure share on apples and $1 - \phi$ is the optimal household expenditure share on bananas. Assuming that $\widehat{\phi}$, the measured expenditure share on apples, is equal to ϕ, the household preference parameter, then the change in utility derived in equation (1.6) is the same as measured growth in real GDP. Restated, if household preferences are such that expenditure shares are constant over time, and all of GDP is consumed in each period (discussed later), then utility in 2001 is greater than utility in 2000 when measured real GDP growth from 2000 to 2001 is positive.

1.1.3 Historical Behavior of Nominal and Real GDP

Detailed data for nominal and real GDP and its components (described later in this chapter) are available in a collection of tables called the National Income and Product Accounts or NIPA. The government statistical agency in charge of collecting data used in the NIPA is the Bureau of Economic Analysis (BEA). The NIPA are available for free download at the BEA's website, www.bea.gov. Click on the "Gross Domestic Product (GDP)" link, then click on the "Interactive Tables: GDP and the National Income and Product Account (NIPA) Historical Tables" link, and then click on the "List of All NIPA Tables" link. The top-line estimates for GDP and its components are in Tables 1.1.5 (nominal) and 1.1.6 (real). Details on the individual components of GDP are available in some of the other tables. In 2007,

---

[7] See footnote 5.

annual nominal GDP was $13,841.3 billion and annual real GDP was
$11,566.8 billion (base year 2000).[8]

One of the interesting properties of real GDP is that it has increased
at roughly a constant rate over the past century. The natural logarithm
of annual real GDP (the solid line) is graphed in Figure 1.1 from 1929,
the first year of the annual NIPA data, to 2007. Also on the figure is
a "trend" line, the dotted line, which represents the path for log real
GDP if log real GDP had increased by a fixed amount in each year
over history.

Note that if trend log real GDP increases by g units in each period,
then the growth rate of trend real GDP increases by $100 * g$ percent in each period. To see this, denote y_t^* as trend real GDP. When
$\ln\left(y_{t+1}^*\right) - \ln\left(y_t^*\right) = g$, this implies:

$$g = \ln\left(y_{t+1}^*\right) - \ln\left(y_t^*\right) = \ln\left(\frac{y_{t+1}^*}{y_t^*}\right)$$

$$= \ln\left(1 + \frac{y_{t+1}^* - y_t^*}{y_t^*}\right)$$

$$\approx \frac{y_{t+1}^* - y_t^*}{y_t^*},$$

where $\left(y_{t+1}^* - y_t^*\right)/y_t^*$ is the rate of growth of trend GDP. The first
two equations are from properties of the natural logarithm. The
last equation is from the first-order Taylor series approximation that
$\ln(1 + z) \approx z$ for z close to zero.[9]

The constant change in trend log GDP shown in the dotted line
in Figure 1.1 is 0.036, implying that the average rate of growth of
real GDP over the entire 1929–2009 period is 3.6 percent per year. As
evidenced by the fact that log real GDP has been below the dotted-line

[8] In the NIPA accounts, real variables (such as real GDP) are reported in units of
"Billions of chained (2000) dollars."
[9] See the appendix for details.

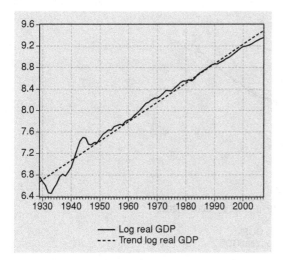

Figure 1.1 Annual log real GDP and "trend" log real GDP, 1929–2007

trend since 1990, the trend rate of growth of real GDP has not been constant over the entire 1929–2007 period.[10] That said, it appears that trend real GDP growth has been about constant since 1973. When we reestimate trend log real GDP for the 1973–2007 period and graph log real GDP alongside its trend over this time period, we uncover quite a tight fit, shown in Figure 1.2. The change in trend log real GDP over the 1973–2007 period is 0.030, implying real GDP increased on average by about 3.0 percent per year since 1973.

Figure 1.3 graphs the natural logarithms of nominal and real GDP together. This figure shows that nominal GDP (dotted line) has increased at a faster rate than real GDP (solid line), especially after 1950. There have been two rather important episodes where prices of goods and services have increased relatively quickly: in the period following World War II, in which wartime price controls were relaxed and the average price of goods and services adjusted upward,

---

[10] We discuss the issue of the measurement of trend log GDP in great detail in Chapter 5.

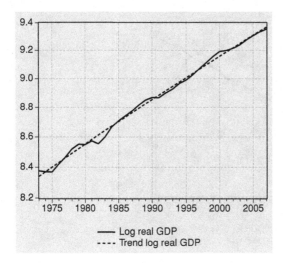

Figure 1.2 Annual log real GDP and trend log real GDP, 1973–2007

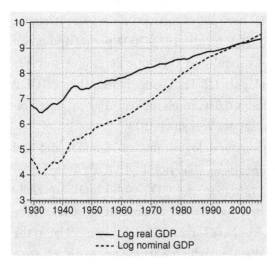

Figure 1.3 Annual log real GDP and log nominal GDP, 1929–2007

and in the 1970s, when policymakers at the Federal Open Market Committee (FOMC) forgot how to control the rate of inflation.

1.1.4 Caveats

In practice, GDP does not measure all of the output produced in the US economy. For example, all work done at home that is non-marketed but still produced (such as child-care, laundry, home-cooked meals, etc.) is not included as GDP. One reason that per-capita GDP of the richest set of countries is much higher than the per-capita GDP of the poorest set of countries – a fact we discuss further in Chapter 2 – is that more goods and services tend to be produced at home rather than purchased in the marketplace in poorer countries.[11]

Second, growth in real GDP only tracks growth in living standards if all of GDP is consumed each period. If some of GDP is set aside as investment, then changes in GDP growth arising solely due to changes in investment rates are not necessarily linked to changes in current living standards. The concepts of consumption and investment are explained in more detail in the next section.

1.2 Components of GDP

As noted earlier, we are not going to separately keep track of all the apples, bananas, computers, etc. that go into GDP. But we will

---

[11] Under reasonable assumptions about how output is produced at home, accounting for the value of output produced at home reduces the gap of income per person between the richest and poorest countries. See S. Parente, R. Rogerson, and R. Wright, 2000, "Homework in Development Economics: Household Production and the Wealth of Nations," *Journal of Political Economy*, vol. 108, pp. 680–687.

keep track of the uses of GDP. Specifically, all of output (GDP) is used somehow, and the standard macroeconomic accounting for how GDP is divided into its uses is:

$$GDP \equiv C + I + G + (X - M). \tag{1.7}$$

(The triple equals sign means "is defined as.") C stands for private consumption; I for private investment; G for government spending (divided into government consumption and government investment for federal, state, and local governments); and $X - M$ for net exports, or exports (X) less imports (M).[12] This is called the "expenditure method" for measuring GDP, since it measures output by keeping track of how output is spent.

Forget the net exports for a second: here's the way to think about the other pieces. We combine capital, labor, and technology to produce output. This output is allocated by households, firms, and the government into government spending (G), private consumption (C), and private investment (I).

1.2.1 Private Consumption

Private consumption, hereafter called consumption, is anything that gives us utility this period, that cannot also give us utility next period. An easy example of consumption is the eating of an apple. When we eat an apple, we receive some utility. Once the apple is fully eaten, it does not provide any more utility.

In future chapters, when we define our theory of household behavior, our utility functions will have consumption as an argument. We will assume that the utility our households receive in period t is

[12] This equation exactly holds for nominal GDP but may not exactly hold for real GDP for relatively unimportant reasons.

explicitly linked to period t consumption. This means that quarter-to-quarter movements of real GDP (inclusive of consumption, investment, government spending, and net exports) will not exactly track quarter-to-quarter changes to utility and welfare, since GDP can change when investment changes, holding consumption constant.

In terms of measurement, sometimes consumption is reasonably easy to measure: haircuts, restaurant meals, electricity used, etc. A few components of consumption are quite tricky to measure, specifically the consumption services generated by a durable good, such as a house. In the case of housing, economists try to measure the value of a flow of non-storable services that housing spins off each period. To explain: houses can last 80 years or more, so we wouldn't want to include the whole value of a house as consumption today – because we know that the same house will provide some consumption services tomorrow. Instead, we try to measure how much it would cost to rent the house for one period. That rental price is counted as the value of consumption of housing services for that house for the current period. For this reason, GDP includes imputed rents to owner-occupied housing as part of consumption.

Unfortunately, the BEA gets the accounting wrong, for lack of a better word, with other durable goods such as cars, furniture, eyeglasses, etc. In the NIPA accounts, the BEA assumes that households consume all the value of these other durable goods in the period in which the purchase occurs, which is clearly incorrect since durable goods provide services over the course of many years. In the case of automobiles, for example, a better measurement system might use leasing rates to determine period-by-period consumption.[13]

---

[13] The BEA knows that it is incorrectly computing the consumption flow from durables. However, it follows the internationally approved standards of National

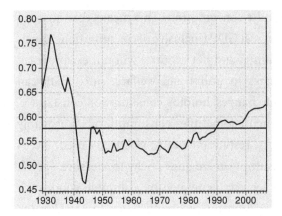

Figure 1.4 Ratio of annual nominal consumption (excluding durables) to annual nominal GDP, 1929–2007

For the past 50 years or so, consumption (excluding the line-item "consumption of durable goods," which, as discussed, is not properly-measured consumption) has accounted for about 58 percent of GDP, shown in Figure 1.4.[14] In 2007, annual nominal consumption exclusive of durables was $8,656.0 billion and annual real consumption exclusive of durables was approximately $7,042 billion (base year 2000).

One of the interesting and important properties of real consumption is that it fluctuates less around its trend than real GDP – using jargon, economists say that consumption is "smoother" than GDP. To show the relative magnitude of the fluctuations, Figure 1.5 plots deviations of log real consumption (exclusive of real durable-goods purchases) from its trend – called "detrended log real consumption" in the graph – alongside deviations of log real GDP from its trend (detrended log real GDP). By graphing the detrended log series, the

Income Accounting known as "SNA 93," and the international body that sets these standards refuses to recognize that cars, furniture, and other durable goods produce services that last longer than one quarter.

[14] The exact average over the 1929–2007 period is 57.7 percent.

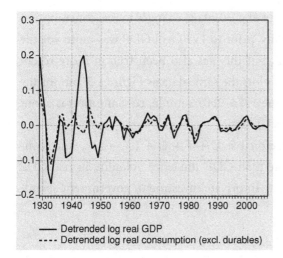

Figure 1.5 Detrended log real consumption (excluding durables) and log real GDP, 1929–2007

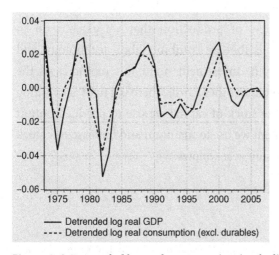

Figure 1.6 Detrended log real consumption (excluding durables) and log real GDP, 1973–2007

graph shows the volatility of percentage changes to real consumption and real GDP.[15] Certainly, prior to 1950 real GDP was more volatile than real consumption, but this has also been true in more recent years as well. Figure 1.6 plots the same data as Figure 1.5, but for the 1973–2007 period. In the 1973–2007 sample, consumption is about 72 percent as volatile as GDP.[16]

Recall that GDP is defined as $C + I + G + (X - M)$. Since consumption is less volatile than GDP, the extra volatility in real GDP must arise from volatility in private investment, government spending, or net exports.

1.2.2 Private Investment

Investment does not provide us with any utility today. Rather, investment is anything that we store away today for the purposes of producing consumption at some point (or at all points) in the future.

A straightforward view of production that we expand on in Chapter 2 of this book is that we combine labor, technology, and capital to produce output. Investment maintains or increases the stock of productive capital. In other words, there is a tight accounting relationship between the stock of capital we use to produce output and the flow of investment we use to maintain and increase our stock of capital. This relationship is as follows:

$$K_{t+1} = K_t - \delta K_t + I_t.$$

---

[15] Both annual log real consumption and annual log real GDP have been detrended using the "HP-Filter" with smoothing parameter $\lambda = 100$. We discuss the HP-Filter and issues relating to the detrending of variables in detail in Chapter 5.

[16] Specifically, the standard deviation of detrended log real consumption (excluding durables) in the 1973–2007 sample is 1.4. The same statistic for detrended log real GDP is 1.9.

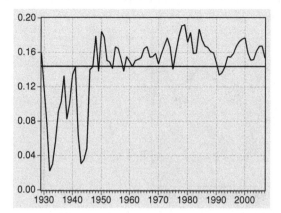

Figure 1.7 Ratio of annual nominal gross private domestic investment to annual nominal GDP, 1929–2007

The above equation says that the stock of capital in period $t+1$, K_{t+1}, is equal to the stock of capital in period t, K_t, less some capital that has depreciated (i.e. become worn out or obsolete during the period) defined as δK_t, plus the flow of any new investment during the period, I_t. The parameter δ represents the depreciation rate on capital.

Figures 1.7 and 1.8 graph the ratio of investment ("gross private domestic investment") to GDP from 1929 to 2007 and detrended log real investment and detrended log real GDP over the sample period 1973–2007.[17] The share of GDP attributable to private investment has been roughly stable since 1950 at about 16 percent; including the pre-1950 data lowers the average investment share to 14 percent. In 2007, annual nominal investment was $2,125.4 billion and annual real investment was $1,825.5 billion (base year 2000). Figure 1.8 shows that even in the relatively stable 1973–2007 period, the standard deviation

---

[17] Detrended log real investment is defined analogously to detrended log real consumption and detrended log real GDP. I omit data prior to 1973 because these data are a more extreme version of the post-1973 data.

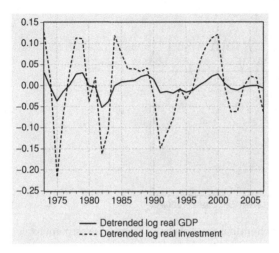

Figure 1.8 Detrended log real gross private domestic investment and detrended log real GDP, 1973–2007

of detrended log investment is about $4\frac{1}{2}$ times more volatile than that of detrended log real GDP.[18]

1.2.3 Government Spending

Government spending in the NIPA is subdivided into spending by the federal government on national defense and non-defense items and spending by state and local governments. The spending itself is further classified as consumption or investment: for details, see NIPA Table 3.9.5, "Government Consumption Expenditures and Gross Investment." Although the share of GDP accounted for by government expenditures has been relatively stable since 1950 at about 20 percent (not shown), the percentage of government expenditures accounted

---

[18] The ratio of the standard deviation of detrended log real investment to detrended log real GDP in the 1973–2007 period is 4.44. As in the case of Figure 1.6, both annual log real GDP and annual log real investment have been detrended using the HP-Filter with smoothing parameter $\lambda = 100$.

Table 1.2 **Annual nominal government expenditures in 2007**		
Federal: national-defense	Consumption	$578.9
	Investment	$81.2
Federal: non-defense	Consumption	$277.2
	Investment	$38.7
State and local	Consumption	$1,365.9
	Investment	$347.9

for by the state and local governments (as compared to the federal government) has varied quite a bit.

Table 1.2 shows how the BEA classifies nominal annual government spending in the NIPA in 2007. Notice that in 2007 state and local consumption accounts for most of government spending.[19] It might seem odd that state and local expenditures account for most of government expenditures, even though the federal government collects quite a bit more in taxes.[20] The reason is that much of the tax revenue and other receipts collected by the federal government is simply transferred back to people via social security or Medicare; it is never actually "spent" by the federal government. This is less true for state and local governments.

The fact that government expenditures, as measured in the NIPA, are not necessarily linked to tax revenues is related to another important point, which is that government expenditures in GDP accounting

[19] Much state and local consumption spending is dedicated to educational spending. According to NIPA Table 3.16, in 2006 state and local governments spent $577 billion on education (elementary, secondary, and higher). A case can be made that this spending is actually investment – the government is educating a work force, and the education itself is a long-term asset that economists call "human capital."

[20] According to NIPA Tables 3.2 (Federal) and 3.3 (State and Local), in 2007 the federal government collected $2,673.5 billion in receipts, and state and local governments collected $1,886.4 billion.

are also not related to government tax surpluses or deficits. Suppose we are in an economy where the government is running a deficit and is financing purchases via some fresh debt in addition to income taxes. Also suppose for simplicity that net exports $(X - M)$ in the economy are zero. Assuming households use what is left of their income to purchase consumption or investment, or to purchase the newly issued government debt, income accounting at the household level looks like:

$$C + [I + B] = [Y - T]. \qquad (1.8)$$

Disposable income, income net of taxes collected by the government, is defined as $Y - T$. This income accounting equation simply says that income net of taxes $(Y - T)$ is either consumed C or saved by households. Households save when they purchase new investment goods I or purchase bonds from the government B. Government bonds are a form of saving by households since the government is committing to repay the bonds, with interest, at some point in the future. In this example, we have assumed, for simplicity, that all new debt that the government issues B is bought by households in the US.

Since we have set $X - M = 0$, we can use equation (1.7) to rewrite the household budget constraint in a way that makes GDP accounting clear. As long as aggregate pre-tax household income Y is equal to GDP, then

$$C + I + [T + B] = Y.$$

Thus, NIPA accounting implies that government spending G is equal to tax revenues raised plus net debt issuance, $T + B$. The fact that the government did not collect enough tax revenue to finance its spending does not affect our accounting of overall government spending.

If you stare at equation (1.8) long enough, you might convince yourself that government deficits B crowd out (replace) private investment I. The thinking might go like this: households decide how much they want to save out of after-tax income, and that household saving is split between private investment I and new government bonds B. So the higher government debt and B are, the lower private investment and I will be. That said, a different view is as follows: there is a fixed amount of output in the aggregate that can be produced in any given year, and the government claims some of that output. If the government claims more of aggregate output for its own use – that is, G increases – that leaves less output for households to spend on either C or I.[21] Because households might like to keep their consumption C roughly constant and smooth – a property of consumption we noticed in the data – then private investment I might decline. In this sense, government purchases might crowd out private investment. But this is not the same as government debt, since government spending can be financed with either debt or taxes.

1.2.4 Net Exports

We discuss trade and net exports in Chapter 4 of the book. For now, I don't have much to say about net exports other than that they allow the sum of C, I, and G to be greater or less than GDP. Recall the GDP accounting equation

$$\text{GDP} \equiv C + I + G + (X - M).$$

Suppose for simplicity that government spending G is zero. Now suppose that $C = \text{GDP}$. This does not imply that investment is

---

[21] This is consistent with a view of production that suggests that, at any given time, the economy-wide resources that can be used for production, capital, and labor are essentially fixed. Thus, if the government wants more missiles (say), then the capital and labor used to make missiles cannot simultaneously be used to make private consumption or investment goods.

zero. Rather, GDP accounting requires that investment, I, is equal to imports less exports $M - X$. In the situation we have described, foreigners (the suppliers of imports) are financing all domestic investment and thus foreigners own claims to the stock of capital in the US. This observation directly follows from the capital-accounting equation,

$$K_{t+1} = K_t - \delta K_t + I_t.$$

Since I_t is financed by non-US residents, they acquire a claim to the stock of capital in the US. Therefore, in this scenario (which is not too far removed from the situation in the US in 2007) (a) consumption is high and (b) net exports are negative. This implies that US residents are selling their stock of capital to finance investment.

When net exports in the United States are negative, as they are now, a lot of opinion pieces in the newspapers suggest that US residents are wasteful and irresponsible. That is, the overwhelming desire for consumption today in the US has led to a big trade deficit, which itself implies that US residents are financing current consumption by selling off wealth (and thus potentially reducing future prosperity). This kind of rhetoric is effective in scaring folks that have a fairly advanced background in economics.

In a sense, this rhetoric is correct – the US is selling assets to finance consumption. But a different and more optimistic story about the health of the US economy, and the responsibility of its consumers, can be told. Suppose that non-US residents want to hold US assets in their portfolio, so much so that they are willing to pay a premium for the assets over and above what US residents are willing to pay for the same assets. Since non-US residents are paying US residents a premium for the assets, US residents are happy to sell the assets to them. However, when the assets are sold, something needs to be bought. This means that in return for the assets that are sold, consumption or investment goods are received in return. In sum, when the United States runs a big trade deficit – meaning $X - M < 0$ – at the same time that its residents are enjoying a lot of consumption and saving relatively little (as was the case in 2007), this is not necessarily indicative of bad things to come for US residents. It could simply mean that non-US residents are demanding US assets at relatively high prices, and when assets are sold, something must be received in return.[22]

1.2.5 Miscellany

Two other minor points to keep in mind:

- Real C, I, G, and $X - M$ are computed in an identical fashion to the apples–bananas example in section 1.1.1. For example, if apples and bananas were two investment goods, then in the examples of section 1.1.1 we would have computed real investment in apples and bananas.
- Equation (1.7) exactly holds for nominal GDP, C, I, G, and $X - M$, but for technical reasons it only approximately holds for the real variables. The gap between real GDP and the sum of real C, I, G, and $X - M$ is reported in line 25 of NIPA Table 1.1.6. As a percentage of real GDP, this gap has been less than 5 percent in the postwar period.

[22] Trade is potentially beneficial whenever two countries have different relative prices for two goods. In this paragraph, I've assumed the implied interest rate on US assets is higher for United States residents than in the rest of the world. Since the interest rate is the price of consumption today relative to consumption in the future (as we show in Chapter 4), any decline in the interest rate on US assets (that is induced by non-US residents purchasing US capital stock and increasing the price of this capital) will be associated with an increase in current consumption of US residents.

1.3 More GDP Accounting

Every time a dollar is spent a dollar is earned. So a different method to calculate GDP involves adding up all the income earned from all sources: this is often called the "income method." In practice, the income method and the expenditure method do not quite equal each other, and the difference is named in the NIPA as "the statistical discrepancy."

As mentioned earlier, macroeconomists model output as being produced using a combination of technology, capital, and labor. For simplicity, it is assumed the technology is freely available to all, and since it is freely provided it earns no income. On the other hand, capital and labor are costly inputs to production. If we view output as being produced using only two costly inputs, it is convenient to try to measure income earned to each of the two inputs separately. Therefore, we will divide all income earned (which is roughly the same as GDP) into two pieces that correspond to our model of production: capital income and labor income.[23]

Dividing income, as it is classified and measured in the NIPA, separately into neat buckets corresponding to capital and labor income is a bit tricky. This is because in the reporting of income in the NIPA, income is not labeled exactly as capital income or labor income. NIPA Table 1.10 (See Figure 1.9) lists the various components of aggregate income. A few line items in this table are straightforward to classify as either capital or labor income. For example, line 2 of this table, "Compensation of employees, paid," represents unambiguous payments to

---

[23] Note that – ignoring the possibility of foreign ownership of capital – households own all the capital and provide all the labor, so after-tax capital income and labor income both accrue to households. In other words, the income variable Y in equation (1.8) refers to the sum of capital and labor income.

Bureau of Economic Analysis
National Income and Product Accounts Table

Table 1.10. Gross Domestic Income by Type of Income
[Billions of dollars]

Today is: 6/24/2008   Last Revised on May 29, 2008   Next Release Date June 26, 2008

Line		2006	2007
1	**Gross domestic income**	**13,212.8**	**13,818.9**
2	**Compensation of employees, paid**	**7,454.8**	**7,888.2**
3	Wage and salary accruals	6,032.2	6,395.7
4	Disbursements	6,024.7	6,373.2
5	To persons	6,015.3	6,363.1
6	To the rest of the world	9.4	10.0
7	Wage accruals less disbursements	7.5	22.5
8	Supplements to wages and salaries	1,422.6	1,492.5
9	**Taxes on production and imports**	**967.3**	**1,008.5**
10	Less: Subsidies [1]	49.7	47.1
11	**Net operating surplus**	**3,225.3**	**3,282.7**
12	Private enterprises	3,239.2	3,297.2
13	Net interest and miscellaneous payments, domestic industries	791.3	837.4
14	Business current transfer payments (net)	90.2	94.2
15	Proprietors' income with inventory valuation and capital consumption adjustments	1,006.7	1,042.6
16	Rental income of persons with capital consumption adjustment	54.5	65.4
17	Corporate profits with inventory valuation and capital consumption adjustments, domestic industries	1,296.4	1,257.7
18	Taxes on corporate income	453.9	466.6
19	Profits after tax with inventory valuation and capital consumption adjustments	842.5	791.0
20	Net dividends	623.1	659.5
21	Undistributed corporate profits with inventory valuation and capital consumption adjustments	219.4	131.5
22	Current surplus of government enterprises [1]	−13.9	−14.5
23	**Consumption of fixed capital**	**1,615.2**	**1,686.6**
24	Private	1,347.5	1,398.7
25	Government	267.7	287.9
	Addendum:		
26	Statistical discrepancy	−18.1	−22.4

Figure 1.9 Bureau of Economic Analysis National Income and Product Accounts Table 1.10: Gross domestic income by type of income

labor. Five of the other lines in the table represent unambiguous payments to capital:[24]

- net interest and miscellaneous payments, domestic industries, line 13
- business current transfer payments (net), line 14
- rental income of persons with capital consumption adjustment, line 16
- corporate profits with inventory valuation and capital consumption adjustments, domestic industries, line 17
- consumption of fixed capital, line 23.

In contrast, the other categories of income on this table are hard to unambiguously classify:

- taxes on production and imports, line 9, less subsidies, line 10
- proprietors' income with inventory valuation and capital consumption adjustments, line 15[25]
- current surplus of government enterprises, line 22
- statistical discrepancy, line 26.

We determine capital's share of income by assuming that capital's share in the ambiguous categories of income is the same as capital's share of income in the overall economy. Denote the economy-wide share of capital income as α. Then, given the categories of unambiguous capital income (lines 13, 14, 16, 17, and 23) and ambiguous income (lines 9, 10, 15, 22, and 26), an estimate of α is:

$$\alpha = \frac{\text{Unambiguous capital income} + \alpha * \text{Ambiguous income}}{\text{Gross domestic income}}$$
$$= \frac{\text{Unambiguous capital income}}{\text{Gross domestic income} - \text{Ambiguous income}} \tag{1.9}$$

[24] This section is taken largely from T. Cooley, and E. Prescott, 1995, "Economic Growth and Business Cycles," in *Frontiers of Business Cycle Research*, ed. T. Cooley, Princeton, NJ: Princeton University Press, pp. 18–19. Those familiar with that book will realize that I am not exactly following the procedure they document.
[25] Proprietors' income sounds like labor payments to a proprietor, but since it takes capital as well as labor to be a proprietor, it is not unambiguous labor income.

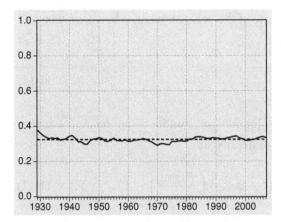

Figure 1.10 Capital's share of income (α), 1929–2007

When we take equation (1.9) to the data, we uncover an estimate of $\alpha = 0.32$ that is fairly constant over history: see Figure 1.10. We will use this estimate of $\alpha = 0.32$ throughout the book.

1.4 Inflation

Inflation does not refer to the level of prices. Inflation is the rate of change of the price level.

The word "inflation" in everyday language is not as tightly defined as GDP. The word inflation can refer to the rate of change of all prices, some prices, or just one price. This is why discussions of inflation can be confusing or wrong.

Going back to our discussion in section 1.1.1, the inflation rate in the price of apples between 2000 and 2001 is easy to define: it is the rate of change of apple prices,

$$\frac{p_{a,2001}}{p_{a,2000}} - 1. \tag{1.10}$$

Likewise, the inflation rate of the price of bananas between 2000 and 2001 is

$$\frac{p_{b,2001}}{p_{b,2000}} - 1. \tag{1.11}$$

The inflation rate on a "basket" or bundle of apples and bananas between 2000 and 2001 is defined as

$$\widehat{\phi}_{2000}\left(\frac{p_{a,2001}}{p_{a,2000}}\right) + \left(1 - \widehat{\phi}_{2000}\right)\left(\frac{p_{b,2001}}{p_{b,2000}}\right) - 1. \tag{1.12}$$

As before, $\widehat{\phi}_{2000}$ is the measured expenditure share on apples and $\left(1 - \widehat{\phi}_{2000}\right)$ is the measured expenditure share on bananas. So the inflation rate on a bundle of goods is defined exactly analogously to the growth rate of real GDP for a bundle of goods – that is, the way that we average price growth across commodities to define an average inflation rate for all goods and services is the same as the way we average quantity growth across commodities to define a growth rate for real GDP.

Equation (1.12) illustrates that not all prices have to increase for the overall rate of inflation to be positive. Imagine that apple prices increase but banana prices fall a little. If the expenditure share on apples is high enough, the increase in the price of apples might more than offset the decrease in the price of bananas, and the inflation rate on the bundle of apples and bananas will increase.

Policymakers tend to look at the rate of change in the price of all consumption items taken together. The most widely followed data on changes in consumer prices is the Consumer Price Index (CPI), produced by the US Department of Labor, Bureau of Labor Statistics (BLS). The BLS samples data from urban consumers (representing about 87 percent of the population). The current CPI release can be found at www.bls.gov/news.release/cpi.htm. The NIPA also produces

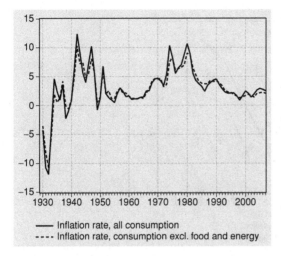

Figure 1.11 Annual inflation rate, all consumption and consumption excl. food and energy, 1930–2007

a price index for all consumption items: See NIPA Table 2.3.4. The NIPA price index is based on underlying BLS data, but growth in the NIPA price index for all consumption items are based on economy-wide expenditure shares that are updated each quarter.[26]

Figure 1.11 plots the annual growth rates of two similar measures of consumer price inflation from the NIPA. The first (solid line) includes all consumption goods including consumer durables, line 1 of NIPA Table 2.3.4. The second (dotted line) excludes food and energy from the bundle, line 23 of NIPA Table 2.3.4. Until very recently, the Federal Reserve appears to have focused on this second measure of inflation when thinking about the course of future monetary policy; as you can see, the two consumer price inflation series track each other closely over long periods of time, but food and energy prices can be

---

[26] In contrast, the expenditure shares in the CPI are updated only every two years. For example, starting with the January 2008 release of the CPI, the expenditure weights are fixed at a 2005–6 base level.

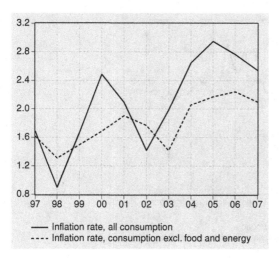

Figure 1.12 Annual inflation rate, all consumption and consumption excl. food and energy, 1997–2007

more volatile, especially at the monthly frequency. Since 2003, the inflation rate for all consumption goods has been about one-half of a percentage point per year higher than the measure that excludes food and energy, shown in Figure 1.12. Recent statements by US policymakers indicate that, relative to previous years, they are paying more attention to the inflation rate for all consumption goods and services and less attention to the inflation measure excluding food and energy.[27] Notice from Figure 1.11 that the inflation rate of consumer prices has almost always been positive since the Second World War.

As we discuss in Chapter 6 of the book, policymakers in the US appear to implicitly focus on consumer price inflation; the rate of change of the price of investment goods appears to receive less consideration. Many investment goods prices have been falling rapidly

---

[27] See, for example, the speech by James Bullard, President of the Federal Reserve Bank of St. Louis, "Remarks on the US Economy and the State of the Housing Sector," made at the Wisconsin School of Business, June 6, 2008. The text of the speech is available at www.stlouisfed.org/news/speeches/2008/06_06_08.html.

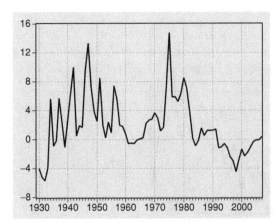

Figure 1.13 Annual inflation rate, investment in equipment and software, 1930–2007

for quite some time – see Figure 1.13 for a graph of the inflation rate of equipment and software (from NIPA Table 1.1.4, line 10), which has been negative in recent years. However, shown in Figure 1.14, the price of one very important investment good, owner-occupied housing, increased very rapidly from 1997 to 2006, and has fallen somewhat since 2007. The inflation rate of housing does not show up in the CPI or the NIPA consumption inflation rate because a house is an investment good. That is, since a house generates services that last many years, the purchase of a house is considered an investment. Instead, the change in rental rates for housing is included as a component in the measurement of consumer price inflation. The rental rate is the price of a unit of housing services for a fixed amount of time (say one year), so it measures the price of the housing services consumed over a one-year period.

With the exception of various sections of Chapters 4 and 6, in the remainder of this book we abstract completely from inflation. There are two reasons for this.

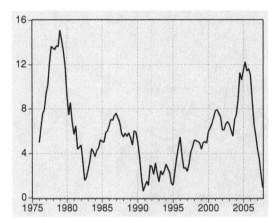

Figure 1.14 Annual inflation rate, owner-occupied housing (from www.ofheo.gov), 1975–2007

- In one sense, inflation is very easy to understand. Suppose that in our economy we only produce and consume apples. Suppose also that we purchase apples with dollar bills. If the government doubles the number of dollar bills in circulation, but the number of apples in the economy is fixed, then the price of an apple in dollars will double. Thus, in this worldview, inflation is ultimately caused by the printing of money, but the inflation rate itself is not correlated with real consumption or production (that is, the consumption or production or apples).
- Second, in a different sense, inflation is very hard to understand. That is, one group of economists argue that at two- to four-year horizons, the overall rate of inflation is correlated with real activity (that is, the production and consumption of apples). A second group argues that no such link exists. And a third group argues that a link exists, but the reason for it is fundamentally different than believed by the first group. Anyway, it seems we will not have consensus on this topic for quite some time, so I pass on the issue entirely.

FURTHER READING

- Quite a lot has been written about the history and construction of GDP, and more generally the National Income and Product Accounts. For more details and some history, I suggest readers start at the BEA's website, specifically www.bea.gov/methodologies/index.htm. Readers may find the articles in the "Concepts" section useful, specifically "A Guide to the National Income and Product Accounts of the United States" (dated September, 2006).

- You may have read or heard about alternatives to GDP that might more closely track changes to human welfare or well-being. You may also have heard about measurement procedures aimed at improving current estimates of GDP. The OECD (Organization for Economic Cooperation and Development) has a working paper on its website on this topic by Boarini *et al.*, 2006, "Alternative Measures of Well-Being," available at www.oecd.org/dataoecd/13/38/36165332.pdf which may serve as a jumping-off point on this topic for interested readers.

- Over the years, the computation of accurate rates of inflation for many different types of goods and services has occupied the attention of a number of serious economists. Since payments from some government programs (such as social security) are indexed to the rate of inflation, any biases – up or down – in the computation of inflation rates are of interest to many people and politicians. In the mid-1990s, the Boskin Commission produced the most widely studied document on biases in the computation of CPI inflation rates (produced by the BLS), and a link to the report is at www.ssa.gov/history/reports/boskinrpt.html. Note that the BLS has since addressed some of the concerns listed in this report.

- There is evidence from different countries and in different time periods that a very high rate of inflation, called "hyperinflation," is destabilizing to a country's economy. Wikipedia's entry on the topic is interesting, and includes a list of countries that have experienced a bout of hyperinflation: see http://en.wikipedia.org/wiki/Hyperinflation.

(H) Homework

1 Definitions:

   a.   What does GDP stand for? Write down and then define the four major expenditure components of GDP.

   b.   Define consumer price inflation. What causes consumer price inflation over long periods of time? Why?

2 Households in Minneapolis pick apples a and bananas b from trees each period. For 2000 and 2001, data on apples picked a, bananas picked b, and the price of apples p_a and the price of bananas p_b in Minneapolis is

Year	a	p_a	b	p_b
2000	25	$1.00	30	$2.50
2001	26	$1.02	31	$2.566

   a.   What is nominal GDP in Minneapolis in 2000 and 2001?

   b.   What is the growth rate of real GDP in Minneapolis from 2000 to 2001?

   c.   What is the inflation rate in Minneapolis from 2000 to 2001?

d.   Suppose that households in Minneapolis have preferences for apples and bananas of

$$\phi \ln(a) + (1.0 - \phi) \ln(b)$$

What do you think ϕ is?

3 Consider an economy where everyone picks apples, bananas, or cherries. The prices and quantities picked of apples, bananas, and cherries for the years 2000, 2001, and 2002 are reported in the table below.

	Apples		Bananas		Cherries	
Year	Price	Quantity	Price	Quantity	Price	Quantity
2000	$10	100	$20	100	$35	200
2001	$11	103	$19	102	$35	200
2002	$12	104	$20	103	$36	206

- What is nominal GDP in each of the years?
- Using the expenditure-share approach, what is the growth rate of real GDP and inflation in each year? NOTE: Do not forget to update the expenditure share.
- Using the growth rates of real GDP you have just computed, what is real GDP in each of the years for GDP in (a) base year 2000 and (b) base year 2002?
- What is the growth rate of real GDP and inflation excluding cherries in each year?

4 Fill in the empty cells:

	Apples		Bananas		Nominal GDP	Real GDP (in $2005)	Ann. Growth Rates in %	
Year	Quan.	Price	Quan.	Price			Real GDP	Infl.
2005	10	$2.00	5	$1.00			NA	NA
2006	11	$2.02	6	$1.05				
2007	12	$2.05	7	$1.12				

5 The country of Fruitcake produces apples and bananas. The people of Fruitcake have time-invariant preferences for pounds of apples a and pounds of bananas b of

$$0.2 \ln (a) + 0.8 \ln (b).$$

a. You have been told that nominal GDP in Fruitcake is $100 in the year 2005, $105 in the year 2006, and $110 in the year 2007. Assuming households maximize utility, and all apples and bananas are consumed in each year, what are nominal expenditures on apples in dollars in 2005, 2006, and 2007?

b. You have been given the following data on the price of one pound of apples p_a and bananas p_b in Fruitcake:

	p_a	p_b
2005	$1.0000	$5.000
2006	$1.0300	$5.100
2007	$1.0815	$5.253

Given the answer to part a., determine the inflation rate and the growth rate of real GDP in Fruitcake between 2005 and 2006 and again between 2006 and 2007.

6 In Fredonia, apples and bananas are produced. Between 1920 and 1921, the expenditure share on apples was 20 percent and the price of apples increased by 50 percent. The overall price level between 1920 and 1921 increased only by 5 percent, however. What happened to the price of bananas in Fredonia between 1920 and 1921?

7 Over the 1947:Q1 through 1996:Q4 period, what is the average of the ratio of nominal investment in residential structures to nominal GDP? What was the average of the ratio from 1997:Q1 through 2007:Q4?

8 According to the NIPA data, approximately what fraction of total income has accrued to capital (as opposed to labor) over the 1929–2007 period?

9 A German friend named Dirk from Stanford gives you a table of income accruing to various sources that he has put together for Germany in 2003. By Dirk's reckoning, German national income in 2003 can be attributed to various sources, such as:

Source	Amount
Capital income	$27
Labor income	$63
Ambiguous income	$10
Total income	$100

Calculate capital's share of income in Germany implied by Dirk's data.

10 Dirk has computed his table of national income and believes that income in Germany in 2007 can be attributed to various sources, such as:

Source	Amount
Capital income	$32
Labor income	$63
Ambiguous income	$5
Total income	$100

Calculate capital's share of income for Germany in 2007.

11 Using annual data on real GDP from the NIPA over the 1973–2007 period, calculate the "output gap,"

$$\ln(GDP_t) - \ln(GDP_t^*)$$

for the years 1982 and 2001. NOTE: To calculate $\ln(GDP_t^*)$, regress $\ln(GDP_t)$ against a constant and a time trend over the 1973–2007 period[28] and assume the fitted value of this regression is exactly equal to $\ln(GDP^*)$.

---

[28] A time trend is a variable that increments by 1 in each period, i.e. is 1 in 1973, 2 in 1974, 3 in 1975, and so forth.

2 | Firms and Growth

O Objectives of this Chapter

In this chapter, we study the behavior of firms, specifically the production of output and optimal use of inputs. We use this theory of firm behavior to understand the sources and causes of growth in developed and developing countries.

We model the output of an average or "representative" firm as the outcome of a Cobb–Douglas production function with technology, capital, and labor as inputs. Technology is assumed to be freely available, but capital and labor are costly inputs. We derive two important properties of this production function: constant returns to scale and declining marginal products. Next, we solve for a firm's profit-maximizing choices of labor and capital where the firm takes as outside of its control the market prices for labor (wage rates) and capital (rental rates). We show that when a firm maximizes its profits, it sets the marginal product of labor equal to the wage rate for labor and sets the marginal product of capital equal to the rental rate on capital.

When all firms in the economy produce output according to a Cobb–Douglas production, we can derive average rates of growth of output and capital in a developed economy with a stable population. Specifically, we show that when the rate of return on capital is constant, output of an economy cannot increase solely by the accumulation of capital. Rather, the level of technology must increase for sustained growth to occur, and further the rate of growth of technology determines the rate of growth of both output and capital. We also use the framework of Cobb–Douglas production to discuss the growth rate of output and capital in less developed economies, and the role of capital income taxes in determining the level of capital, output, and wages.

In the final section of the chapter, we discuss measurement of the three inputs of the production function, capital, labor, and technology.

We show that the capital-output ratio of the United States has been roughly constant over history, in accordance with the predictions of theory.

2.1 Cobb–Douglas Production

We start with the assumption that real output in period t, Y_t, is produced by firms using a combination of three inputs: period t technology, which we label as the variable z_t, the real stock of capital in place as of period t, labeled as K_t, and labor used in production in period t, labeled as L_t.

For simplicity, we assume firms produce one good called "output," and, given technology, they only require as inputs homogeneous (identical) capital and homogeneous labor. Obviously, a crane is different than a computer, and people bring various different skills to the labor market. We make the assumptions of homogeneous capital and labor inputs not because we believe these assumptions to be true, but because they enable us to write down a simple model for aggregate output from which we can derive intuition for how the economy functions. If we were to add more realism, the model would be more difficult to manage and solve, but our intuition for how the economy functions might not profoundly change.

It might appear as if we are ignoring important inputs such as metals, minerals, and energy. However, we haven't ignored the production of these intermediate inputs. It takes capital and labor to extract copper from a mine or oil from a field. When copper is combined with some labor and more capital, we can make copper pipes for plumbing; or, when oil is added to an airplane, with more capital (the airplane) and labor (the pilots, flight-attendants, etc.) we produce air travel. So, in thinking about the production of the final output (copper pipes or air travel), we simply add all the capital and labor services involved in the production of the intermediate inputs to the services from capital and labor used in transforming the intermediate inputs to final output.

The specific mathematical production function that we will use to link output to the inputs is

$$Y_t = z_t K_t^\alpha L_t^{1-\alpha}. \tag{2.1}$$

The parameter α is assumed to be fixed over time, and it is a number between 0 and 1: $0 < \alpha < 1$ and $0 < (1 - \alpha) < 1$. Equation (2.1) is called a Cobb–Douglas production function.[1] The Cobb–Douglas production function has two important properties that we will explore in some detail: constant returns to scale and declining marginal products.

2.1.1 Constant Returns to Scale

Constant returns to scale means that, holding z (technology) constant, if we double K (capital) and double L (labor) then Y (output) doubles. This implies that if we assume that every firm has access to the same level of z, and production is Cobb–Douglas, then we can pretend that there is only one firm in the US economy.

To explain: suppose there are two firms in the US economy, each employing the same amount of capital and labor. Then aggregate output is

$$Y_t = z_t K_t^\alpha L_t^{1-\alpha} + z_t K_t^\alpha L_t^{1-\alpha}$$
$$= 2 * z_t K_t^\alpha L_t^{1-\alpha}$$
$$= z_t (2 * K_t)^\alpha (2 * L_t)^{1-\alpha},$$

---

[1] See C. W. Cobb and P. H. Douglas, 1928, "A Theory of Production," *American Economic Review*, vol. 8, pp. 139–165.

where the last equality comes from the identity that $2^\alpha * 2^{1-\alpha} = 2$. These equations tell us that the output of two small firms using Cobb–Douglas production is the same as the output of one firm that is twice as large.

With the assumption of Cobb–Douglas production, and the assumption of perfect competition, we can act as if there is only one firm – a representative firm – in the US economy.

The assumption of perfect competition is important because we will assume later in this chapter that each firm takes the price of its inputs – the market rental rate on capital and the market wage rate on labor – as given and outside of its control. This assumption is not controversial in the case of capital, since (conditional on capital structure and earnings prospects) firms cannot dictate to investors the price of their stock or debt. The assumption seems less valid in the case of labor, since there are more than a few locations in which employment is dominated by one or two major firms, and these firms may be able to dictate wages. However, as long as labor is mobile, at least over long periods of time, then these firms will have to eventually act as if wages are set outside of their control.[2]

2.1.2 Declining Marginal Products

Intuitively, the marginal product of any particular input into production is the extra amount of output that is produced if that input is increased by one unit, holding all other inputs into production

---

[2] I have some personal experience with firms that have tried to ignore market wages. In 1999 and 2000, the Federal Reserve Board in Washington, DC, did not adjust pay for economists with a few years of experience when the market wage for these economists was increasing quite rapidly. I quit the Federal Reserve for this reason in October, 2000. Pay eventually increased, and I returned to the Federal Reserve Board in 2002.

fixed. Specifically, the marginal product of capital is the derivative of the production function with respect to capital, holding the labor and technology inputs fixed. Similarly, the marginal product of labor is the derivative of the production function with respect to labor, holding the capital and technology inputs fixed.

Given how we have defined our production function, the marginal product of capital and labor are as follows:

$$\text{Marginal product of capital} = \alpha * z_t K_t^{\alpha-1} L_t^{1-\alpha} \qquad (2.2)$$

$$\text{Marginal product of labor} = (1 - \alpha) * z_t K_t^{\alpha} L_t^{-\alpha}. \qquad (2.3)$$

Using the properties of exponents, equations (2.2) and (2.3) can be rewritten as

$$\text{Marginal product of capital} = \alpha * z_t \left(\frac{L_t}{K_t}\right)^{1-\alpha} \qquad (2.4)$$

$$\text{Marginal product of labor} = (1 - \alpha) * z_t \left(\frac{K_t}{L_t}\right)^{\alpha}. \qquad (2.5)$$

Since both $\alpha > 0$ and $(1 - \alpha) > 0$, equation (2.4) shows that the marginal product of capital declines as the level of K_t is increased (holding labor L_t and technology z_t constant). Similarly, equation (2.5) shows that the marginal product of labor declines as the level of L_t is increased, holding capital K_t and technology z_t constant.

2.2 Profit Maximization

The firm's objective is to maximize profits. Profits are revenues – output, in this case – less the total cost of the inputs:

$$\text{profits} = Y_t - r_t * K_t - w_t * L_t$$

$$= z_t K_t^{\alpha} L_t^{1-\alpha} - r_t * K_t - w_t * L_t. \qquad (2.6)$$

Firms maximize profits by choosing the amount of capital and labor to use in production. In the above equation, r_t is the period t market-determined rental rate on capital (before depreciation and capital income taxes) and w_t is the period t market-determined wage rate on labor (before labor income taxes). Each firm takes the prices of its inputs, r_t and w_t, as given and independent of its decisions.

Notice that the price of output and capital has been normalized to equal 1.0. A more general version of (2.6) would include relative prices: for example, the price per unit of a firm's output may not be the same as the price per unit of its capital. However, we will assume throughout that all firms make the same output, and that this output can be costlessly subdivided into investment (which adds to capital) or consumption. This means that there is only one good produced in the economy, and since there is only one good, there is only one price. We arbitrarily normalize this price to 1.0.

In addition, we specify that the price of this one good in every period is 1.0, which is equivalent to saying that the inflation rate is *zero*. We make this assumption so that we can work with real variables in this chapter: output denotes real output, and the capital stock in production is the real stock of capital. Likewise, our rental rate of capital and wage rate on labor are going to be in real units. The gap between the real rental rate and the nominal rental rate is the inflation rate, and since the inflation rate is zero, the real and nominal rental rates are the same.

2.2.1 Optimal Capital

In the appendix, we show that a hump-shaped function – like our profit function – is maximized when the derivatives of that function are set to zero. Therefore, the optimal amount of capital – holding the level of technology z_t and labor input L_t constant – is determined by setting the derivative of the profit function with respect to K_t equal to zero. This derivative is

$$\alpha * z_t K_t^{\alpha-1} L_t^{1-\alpha} - r_t = 0. \tag{2.7}$$

As already noted, $\alpha z_t K_t^{\alpha-1} L_t^{1-\alpha}$ is the marginal product of capital because it expresses how much output will increase if capital increases by one unit.[3] Equation (2.7) therefore satisfies the restriction that the marginal revenue from an additional unit of capital – the extra output gained from one additional unit of capital – is exactly equal to the marginal cost of an additional unit of capital, r_t. In other words, the marginal benefit of capital is equated to its marginal cost.

Now, multiply (2.7) by K_t and rearrange terms. This gives the following relationship:

$$K_t * \alpha * z_t K_t^{\alpha-1} L_t^{1-\alpha} = r_t * K_t \tag{2.8}$$

$$\alpha * Y_t = r_t * K_t. \tag{2.9}$$

Equation (2.9) follows from (2.8) because $K_t * z_t K_t^{\alpha-1} L_t^{1-\alpha} = z_t K_t^{\alpha} L_t^{1-\alpha}$ which is equal to Y_t. Equation (2.9) states that when firms optimize, the amount they spend on capital services ($r_t * K_t$) is equal to a constant fraction α of the value of firm output Y_t. Now, since every dollar spent is a dollar earned, the amount paid for capital services by firms in the aggregate must be equal to capital income received in the aggregate. We learned from Chapter 1 that capital income accounts for about 32 percent of total income. This gives us an estimate of α for use in our production function: 0.32. Economists call α the "capital share" in production.

Also note that because α is a constant parameter in the production function, equation (2.9) implies that capital income is a constant

[3] Recall, this is the very definition of a derivative.

fraction of total income. This result appears to be roughly validated by the NIPA data, as shown in Figure 1.10.

2.2.2 Optimal Labor

To derive firms' optimal decision for the amount of labor to employ, we set the derivative of the profit function with respect to the labor input equal to zero, holding technology and capital constant:

$$(1 - \alpha) * z_t K_t^{\alpha} L_t^{-\alpha} - w_t = 0. \tag{2.10}$$

Summarizing (2.10), profit maximization requires the real pre-tax wage (that is, the wage prior to labor income taxes being collected from the worker) be equal to the marginal product of labor. Multiply both sides of equation (2.10) by L_t and rearrange terms to yield

$$(1 - \alpha) * Y_t = L_t * w_t. \tag{2.11}$$

This equation states that firms' payment to labor – which, in the aggregate, will equal total labor income that is received by workers – is a constant $(1 - \alpha)$ fraction of the value of output. Economists call $(1 - \alpha)$ the "labor share" in production. Since we have estimated α to be 0.32, we estimate the labor share in production to be 0.68.

2.2.3 Optimal Profits

We noted in equation (2.6) that profits are defined as $Y_t - r_t * K_t - w_t * L_t$. But, $r_t * K_t = \alpha * Y_t$ from equation (2.9) and $w_t * L_t = (1 - \alpha) * Y_t$ from equation (2.11). So, $Y_t - r_t * K_t - w_t * L_t = 0$. In other words, firms make no economic profits given our assumptions.

This may seem silly to you: of course firms make profits! But economic profits are not the same thing as accounting profits. If a person invests in a firm, that person requires a certain rate of return on the investment. The firm sells some stuff, subtracts the payments to labor and a depreciation allowance, and calls the rest profits or (in the parlance of accounting) "retained earnings." But these accounting profits are a payment to the investor for loaning capital to the firm. In other words, accounting profits are rental payments to equity investors for providing the firm with capital.

2.3 Growth Accounting

A tenet in economics is that productivity growth is essential for long-lasting changes in welfare. The "average product of labor" is defined as the amount of output that is produced divided by the amount of labor used to produce that output.

$$\text{Average product of labor} = \frac{Y_t}{L_t}.$$

When the labor input is measured as the total amount of hours worked, the average product of labor is called "output per hour." The average product of labor may also be called "labor productivity."

Now, note that equation (2.11) – the equation that defines a firm's optimal labor input – can be rewritten as

$$(1 - \alpha) * \frac{Y_t}{L_t} = w_t$$

$$(1 - \alpha) * \text{Average Product of Labor} = w_t. \tag{2.12}$$

Equation (2.12) states that the pre-tax wage rate on labor is proportional to labor productivity. Wages increase only when labor productivity increases.

How is productivity linked to technology? Denote output in 2000 as Y_{2000}, technology in 2000 as z_{2000} and the capital and labor inputs in 2000 as K_{2000} and L_{2000}. Then

$$Y_{2000} = z_{2000} K_{2000}^{\alpha} L_{2000}^{1-\alpha}.$$

Now suppose that between 2000 and 2001 the technology input doubles but the capital and labor inputs remain fixed at their 2000 levels:

$$Y_{2001} = z_{2001} K_{2001}^{\alpha} L_{2001}^{1-\alpha}$$

$$= 2 * z_{2000} K_{2000}^{\alpha} L_{2000}^{1-\alpha}$$

$$= 2 * Y_{2000}.$$

Given the labor input did not change and output doubled, in this example the average product of labor doubled between 2000 and 2001. And, via equation (2.12), this means that the pre-tax wage rate also doubled between 2000 and 2001.

Ultimately, the growth in real output is determined by growth in technology z. Let's write down our production function again for periods t and $t + 1$, but this time take the natural logarithm of both the left-hand and right-hand sides:

$$\ln(Y_{t+1}) = \ln(z_{t+1}) + \alpha \ln(K_{t+1}) + (1 - \alpha) \ln(L_{t+1})$$

$$\ln(Y_t) = \ln(z_t) + \alpha \ln(K_t) + (1 - \alpha) \ln(L_t).$$

Now, subtract the natural logarithm of population from each side of each equation, denoted $\ln(N_{t+1})$ and $\ln(N_t)$ for periods $t + 1$ and t respectively. We do this to understand the causes of changes to output on a per-person or "per-capita" basis. We will use lower-case letter to define our per-capita variables: denote per-capita output in period t as y_t, the per-capita stock of capital as k_t, and the per-capita labor input as l_t, with $t + 1$ defined analogously. Using these definitions, the equations above become

$$\ln(y_{t+1}) = \ln(z_{t+1}) + \alpha \ln(k_{t+1}) + (1 - \alpha) \ln(l_{t+1})$$

$$\ln(y_t) = \ln(z_t) + \alpha \ln(k_t) + (1 - \alpha) \ln(l_t).$$

Note that we have used the properties of constant returns to scale to make this transformation:

$$y_t = \frac{Y_t}{N_t} = \frac{1}{N_t} * z_t K_t^{\alpha} L_t^{1-\alpha} = z_t \left(\frac{K_t}{N_t}\right)^{\alpha} \left(\frac{L_t}{N_t}\right)^{1-\alpha} = z_t k_t^{\alpha} l_t^{1-\alpha}.$$

Subtracting period t from period $t+1$ and using the properties of the natural logarithm gives us

$$\ln\left(\frac{y_{t+1}}{y_t}\right) =$$
$$\ln\left(\frac{z_{t+1}}{z_t}\right) + \alpha \ln\left(\frac{k_{t+1}}{k_t}\right) + (1-\alpha) \ln\left(\frac{l_{t+1}}{l_t}\right).$$

Now use the trick of adding and subtracting 1.0 within each of the parentheses above to yield

$$\ln\left(1 + \frac{y_{t+1} - y_t}{y_t}\right) =$$
$$\ln\left(1 + \frac{z_{t+1} - z_t}{z_t}\right) + \alpha \ln\left(1 + \frac{k_{t+1} - k_t}{k_t}\right)$$
$$+ (1-\alpha) \ln\left(1 + \frac{l_{t+1} - l_t}{l_t}\right).$$

After using the approximations discussed in the appendix, this becomes

$$\frac{y_{t+1} - y_t}{y_t} =$$
$$\left(\frac{z_{t+1} - z_t}{z_t}\right) + \alpha \left(\frac{k_{t+1} - k_t}{k_t}\right) + (1-\alpha) \left(\frac{l_{t+1} - l_t}{l_t}\right). \qquad (2.13)$$

The left-hand side is the growth rate of real per-capita output. The right-hand side has three components: the growth rate of technology, $\left(\frac{z_{t+1} - z_t}{z_t}\right)$, α times the growth rate of the real per-capita stock of capital, $\alpha\left(\frac{k_{t+1} - k_t}{k_t}\right)$, and $(1-\alpha)$ times the growth rate of the per-capita labor input, $(1-\alpha)\left(\frac{l_{t+1} - l_t}{l_t}\right)$.

So how does real output per person in an economy increase? Real output can increase through growth in technology, growth in the real per-capita capital stock, or growth in the per-capita labor input. The importance of each of these inputs differs when comparing the sources of growth of developed countries to growth in developing countries.

2.3.1 Growth in Developed Countries

We show later in this chapter that in the United States, since about 1950 and perhaps earlier, the fraction of total available time spent working has been roughly constant on a per-capita basis.[4] Further, a person's feasible labor input is bounded; after all, unless we forego sleep we can work no more than 16 hours a day. For these reasons, we will assert that an economy's real GDP cannot sustainably increase via sustained growth in the per-capita labor input.

So this means that for mature economies, real per-capita output can sustainably increase either through sustained growth in technology or sustained growth in the per-capita stock of capital.

But it turns out that in a mature economy the per-capita stock of capital is bounded: for any given and fixed level of the labor input and technology, the stock of capital will not increase past a certain limit. To see this refer to equation (2.13) and hold the level of the technology input and the per-capita labor input fixed such that there is no growth in these two variables. When technology and labor are held fixed, this growth accounting equation dictates that the growth rate of real output is equal to α times the growth rate of the real per-capita stock of capital. Since $0 < \alpha < 1$, as capital increases, holding l_t and z_t fixed, y_t/k_t will decline.

---

[4] Although female labor force participation rates have increased, male participation rates have declined and disability rates have increased. These effects net out.

Now, take equation (2.9), the optimality condition for a firm's use of capital, and divide both sides by K_t:

$$\alpha * \frac{Y_t}{K_t} = r_t. \tag{2.14}$$

Holding labor and technology fixed, as capital increases Y_t/K_t declines. At some point, $\alpha * Y_t/K_t$ will be less than the rental rate on capital r_t. Since the rental rate is linked to households' required after-tax return on savings (discussed later in this chapter), at some point households stop investing in capital because the rate of return on additional investment is too low.

To sum up: sustained growth in the per-capita labor input is impossible, and sustained growth in the per-capita stock of capital, holding labor and technology fixed, yields after-tax rates of return on capital that are too low for households to accept. Thus, sustained growth in real GDP and real wages can only be achieved through sustained growth in technology.

2.3.2 Balanced Growth

In the postwar period, the US has been on a "balanced-growth path." On a balanced-growth path,

- real interest rates (the pre-tax pre-depreciation marginal product of capital) are trendless;
- the per-capita labor input is trendless;
- output, consumption, investment, and capital all increase at the same rate;
- the rate of growth of output, consumption, investment, and capital is intrinsically linked to the rate of growth of technology.

In Chapter 1, we showed that the consumption-output and investment-output ratios have been trendless, or close to it, since about 1950. Later in this chapter, we show that the per-capita labor input and capital-output ratio have also been trendless in this period.

The key features of a balanced-growth path can be understood by studying equations (2.13) and (2.14). Suppose that output and capital increase at the same rate. Equation (2.14) says that r_t is trendless. Now, refer back to equation (2.13). Denote the growth rate of per-capita output as g_y, the growth rate of technology as g_z, the growth rate of the per-capita stock of capital as g_k and the growth rate of the per-capita labor input as g_l, such that (2.13) can be rewritten as

$$g_y = g_z + \alpha * g_k + (1 - \alpha) * g_l.$$

Suppose the per-capita labor input does not increase at all, such that $g_l = 0$. Given a growth rate of technology g_z, we can now solve for the growth rate of per-capita output when this is equal to the growth rate of capital ($g_y = g_k$):

$$g_k = g_z + \alpha * g_k$$
$$g_k = \frac{g_z}{1 - \alpha}.$$

Given a growth rate of technology g_z, we know that in balanced growth the per-capita stock of capital and per-capita output both increase at rate $g_z/(1 - \alpha)$.

Now consider GDP accounting, but for simplicity ignore government spending and net exports such that in the aggregate

$$Y_t = C_t + I_t.$$

New investment and changes in the stock of capital are linked by accounting:

$$I_t = K_{t+1} - K_t(1 - \delta),$$

where δ is the constant depreciation rate on capital. Substituting in the capital-stock accounting equation into the GDP accounting equation yields:

$$Y_t = C_t + K_{t+1} - K_t(1 - \delta).$$

Divide both sides by Y_t and use the trick that $1/Y_t = (1/Y_{t+1}) * (Y_{t+1}/Y_t)$:

$$1 = \frac{C_t}{Y_t} + \left(\frac{K_{t+1}}{Y_{t+1}}\right)\left(\frac{Y_{t+1}}{Y_t}\right) - \left(\frac{K_t}{Y_t}\right)(1 - \delta). \qquad (2.15)$$

In balanced growth, the capital-output ratio (K_{t+1}/Y_{t+1} and K_t/Y_t), the growth rate of output (Y_{t+1}/Y_t), and the depreciation rate (δ) are all constant. Since the number 1 and the depreciation rate δ are also constants, equation (2.15) shows that the consumption-output ratio must also be constant in a balanced growth environment. Now return to the GDP accounting equation and divide both sides by Y_t such that:

$$1 = \frac{C_t}{Y_t} + \frac{I_t}{Y_t}.$$

Since the consumption-output ratio is a constant, the investment-output ratio must also be constant.

Summing up, in a balanced-growth environment, interest rates are trendless, implying that capital and output increase at the same rate (which is determined by the rate of growth of technology). When capital and output increase at the same rate, GDP accounting implies that the consumption-output and investment-output ratios are constant.

2.3.3 Growth in Developing Countries

In a country that is not fully developed, real GDP can increase because (a) the per-capita labor input increases (as existing workers switch from work that is not counted towards GDP into market work), (b) the per-capita stock of capital increases (as firms and households build new plants and equipment), or (c) technology increases. Consider the case of China, a country that has developed very rapidly over the past 30 years. In China's case, all three of these events have occurred. The per-capita labor input has likely increased as many households have transitioned from home production (that yields output not counted towards GDP) to market-based production. Technology used in production may have increased and be increasing in China as it has opened up its borders and allowed foreign investment and management expertise to make output more efficiently. And the per-capita stock of capital has increased and is increasing.

In countries that are "under-capitalized," the real rate of return on capital is quite high, which serves to attract investors, investment, and additional capital. Rewrite equation (2.7) as:

$$\alpha * z_t \left(\frac{L_t}{K_t} \right)^{1-\alpha} = r_t.$$

When the labor input L_t is big and the capital stock K_t is small – as was the case for China 30 years ago – then the return on an additional unit of capital is going to be quite high – higher than households' required pre-tax and pre-depreciation rental rate on capital, r_t.

Explaining China's exceptional growth over the past 30 years is therefore straightforward: the growth rate of real GDP per capita in China was high because the labor force moved from home-based work to market-based work, and the per-capita stock of capital increased because the after-tax and after-depreciation rate of return on investment in China was higher than that of other countries. At some point, possibly soon, China will be a "mature" economy: its labor force will largely have finished its transition from home- to market-based work, and the rate of return on additional investments in capital will be the same as the worldwide rate. When this occurs, the growth rate of real per-capita GDP in China will likely be the same as in that of the US, and in both cases the growth rate of real per-capita GDP will ultimately be determined by the growth rate of technology, as is the case in an environment of balanced growth.

We expand on this idea in the next section.

2.3.4 Barriers to Growth

The first column of Table 2.1 shows per-capita real GDP in constant US\$2000 for the 10 poorest and 10 richest countries as of 1973.[5] The second column shows annualized growth in real per-capita GDP from 1973 to 2003, the last year of available data for many countries.[6] Three facts emerge from this table. First, the poorest countries are incredibly poor. As of 1973, GDP per capita of the richest 10 countries was more than 30 times that of the poorest 10 countries. To put the size of this gap in perspective, as of 1973 each US resident produced as much market output in one day as each Malawi resident produced in one month. Second, with the exception of China, over the 1973–2003 period, the level of real per-capita GDP of the poorest countries did not catch up to the level of real per-capita GDP of the richest countries. Real per-capita GDP growth averaged 1.7 percent per year for the richest countries and 1.5 percent per year for the poorest countries

---

[5] The data on real GDP per capita, with real GDP for foreign countries converted to US dollars using "purchasing power parity," can be downloaded for all years over the 1950–2004 period from http://pwt.econ.upenn.edu/php_site/pwt_index.php. These data are made available by A. Heston, R. Summers, and B. Aten, 2006, Penn World Table Version 6.2, Center for International Comparisons of Production, Income and Prices at the University of Pennsylvania, September.

[6] The year 1973 is chosen as a start date in this table to be consistent with data that are shown in Chapter 1.

Table 2.1 **Real per-capita (PC) GDP (constant US$2000) in 1973 and 2003, and growth in real PC GDP 1973–2003, 10 poorest and 10 richest countries as of 1973**

Country*	Real PC GDP 1973	2003	Growth in real PC GDP 1973–2003**
Bhutan	$250	$934	4.5%
Ethiopia	$503	$688	1.0%
North Korea	$542	$1,429	3.3%
China	$561	$4,970	7.5%
Tanzania	$572	$912	1.6%
Malawi	$593	$771	0.9%
Guinea-Bissau	$631	$584	−0.3%
Mali	$638	$1,184	2.1%
Burkina Faso	$692	$1,071	1.5%
Cambodia	$763	$580	−0.9%
Average, bottom 10 (1973)	$574	$1,312	2.1%
Germany	$15,218	$25,188	1.7%
Australia	$15,944	$27,872	1.9%
New Zealand	$15,947	$22,195	1.1%
Canada	$16,034	$27,845	1.9%
Netherlands	$16,294	$26,157	1.6%
Sweden	$16,470	$26,136	1.6%
Denmark	$18,126	$27,970	1.5%
Luxembourg	$19,305	$49,262	3.2%
United States	$19,552	$34,875	1.9%
Switzerland	$23,074	$28,792	0.7%
Average, top 10 (1973)	$17,596	$29,629	1.7%

* The data underlying these estimates are available at http://pwt.econ.upenn.edu/php_site/pwt_index.php. See text for a full citation. Bahamas, Bermuda, Brunei, Gabon, Kuwait, Qatar, Saudi Arabia, and the UAE are excluded from the richest 10 countries as of 1973.

** Annualized percent per year growth in real GDP per capita.

excluding China (not shown), 2.1 percent per year including China. Third, despite 30 years of relatively fast growth, as of 2003 China was still a relatively poor country. In 2003, per-capita real GDP was seven times larger in the United States than in China.

It might appear that the gap between the richest and poorest countries narrowed between 1973 and 2003, since the ratio of GDP per-capita of the richest and poorest 10 countries as of 1973 fell from 31 times ($17,596/$574) in 1973 to 23 times ($29,629/$1,312) in 2003. It turns out that the gap between real per-capita GDP of the most productive and least productive countries actually widened between 1973 and 2003. The reason is that the set of richest and poorest countries changed between 1973 and 2003. Table 2.2 presents the same information as in Table 2.1, except it shows the data for the top 10 richest and poorest countries ranked as of 2003. Table 2.2 shows that as of 2003 the per-capita GDP of the richest 10 countries was more than 52 times ($31,410/$599) that of the poorest 10 countries.

A comparison of Tables 2.1 and 2.2 shows that the relative rankings of countries has changed over time. Austria, Hong Kong, Ireland, and Norway displaced Germany, Netherlands, New Zealand, and Sweden from the top 10 richest countries. Remarkably, the identity of 7 of the 10 poorest countries changed between 1973 and 2003. The identity of most of the bottom 10 countries changed between 1973 and 2003 because GDP per capita increased for almost all of the bottom 10 countries ranked as of 1973, but GDP per capita contracted over the 1973–2003 period for all but one of the poorest 10 countries, ranked as of 2003.

With the exception of the countries with economies that have been destroyed by war, the data in Tables 2.1 and 2.2 represent an unsolved puzzle for economists. To explain: if all countries have access to the same technology, then poor countries have low output on a per-capita basis because workers do not have much capital to use in production.

Table 2.2 **Real per-capita (PC) GDP (constant US$2000) in 1973 and 2003, and growth in real PC GDP, 1973–2003, 10 poorest and 10 richest countries as of 2003**

Country*	Real PC GDP 1973	2003	Growth in real PC GDP 1973–2003**
Liberia	$2,143	$342	−5.9%
Congo, Dem. Rep.	$1,537	$438	−4.1%
Cambodia	$763	$580	−0.9%
Guinea-Bissau	$631	$584	−0.3%
Afghanistan	$2,113	$588	−4.2%
Eritrea	NA	$611	NA
Somalia	$1,379	$683	−2.3%
Ethiopia	$503	$688	1.0%
Sierra Leone	$1,318	$713	−2.0%
Madagascar	$1,315	$759	−1.8%
Average, bottom 10 (2003)	$1,300	$599	−2.3%
Austria	$14,806	$27,567	2.1%
Hong Kong	$8,794	$27,658	3.9%
Canada	$16,034	$27,845	1.9%
Australia	$15,944	$27,872	1.9%
Denmark	$18,126	$27,970	1.5%
Ireland	$8,823	$28,248	4.0%
Switzerland	$23,074	$28,792	0.7%
Norway	$15,030	$34,011	2.8%
United States	$19,552	$34,875	1.9%
Luxembourg	$19,305	$49,262	3.2%
Average, top 10 (2003)	$15,949	$31,410	2.4%

* The data underlying these estimates are available at http://pwt.econ.upenn.edu/php_site/pwt_index.php. See text for a full citation. Bermuda, Macao, Qatar, and the UAE are excluded from the richest 10 countries as of 2003.
** Annualized percent per year growth in real GDP per capita.

Since the marginal product of capital is $\alpha z_t (L_t/K_t)^{1-\alpha}$, the return to investment in capital in countries with a large quantity of labor and not much capital should be high, since L_t is high and K_t is low. If capital is deployed to projects where it earns the highest rate of return, then poor countries should quickly receive large capital inflows from outside investors. The additional capital should raise the per-capita output of poor countries, and the per-capita output of poor countries should quickly catch up to that of rich countries.

In other words, the question economists ask is: why isn't real per-capita GDP of poor countries increasing more rapidly?

One explanation for the lack of fast growth of the poorest countries is that the tax rate on capital income may differ across countries, either explicitly (such as differences in tax rates on capital gains or dividends) or implicitly (such as theft, bribery, and corruption). The high tax rate on capital discourages the inflow of new capital, and keeps real per-capita GDP low in poor countries.

To understand how the tax rate on capital affects the level of real GDP, suppose that there is a worldwide market for capital, and the world-required real rate of return on capital, after taxes and depreciation, is 6 percent.[7] The rate of return on capital that households receive, denoted $\widehat{r}_t$, is equal to the rental rate on capital paid by firms less depreciation and capital income taxes:

$$\widehat{r}_t = (1 - \tau_k)(r_t - \delta). \tag{2.16}$$

r_t is the rental rate on capital that is paid by firms (as discussed throughout this chapter), δ is the depreciation rate on capital, and τ_k is the tax rate on capital income and it includes both explicit taxes and implicit taxes.

---

[7] Remember, we are assuming throughout this chapter that the inflation rate is zero.

Equation (2.16) implies that we can rewrite the pre-tax and pre-depreciation rental rate on capital that is paid by firms, r_t, as a function of the rate of depreciation, the tax rate on capital income, and $\widehat{r}_t$ as

$$r_t = \frac{\widehat{r}_t}{1 - \tau_k} + \delta. \tag{2.17}$$

Here is a way to visualize how r_t is set in equilibrium: households demand a certain after-tax and after-depreciation return on capital. Given tax and depreciation rates, the required after-tax return dictates the rental rate on capital that firms pay, r_t. When firms maximize profit they employ capital until the point at which r_t, their marginal cost for an additional unit of capital, is equal to the marginal product of capital.

To run through an example of how (2.16) might work in practice, suppose you loan $100 worth of computer equipment to a firm for a year. That firm pays you $17.50 for use of the capital during the year, which is its marginal product of that $100 worth of capital. However, the computer equipment depreciates during the course of the year and is only worth $94.50 once the equipment is returned to you. So your pre-tax capital income net of depreciation is $17.50 − $5.50 = $12.00. Now suppose that your capital income (net of a depreciation allowance) is taxed at an average rate of 50 percent. Your after-tax capital income is $(1 − 0.50) * \$12.00 = \$6.00$. So your $100 loan, after taxes and depreciation, returned 6 percent, $6.

Now, let's use these formulas and ideas to compare two economies that have the same labor input and the same technology, but one economy has a 60 percent tax rate on capital income and one economy has a 40 percent tax rate on capital income. Since the economies are identical (except for the tax rates), for simplicity set the technology level z_t and labor-input level L_t equal to 1.0 in both places. This gives us that output in both countries is equal to

$$Y_t = K_t^{\alpha}.$$

The marginal product of capital is

$$r_t = \alpha * K_t^{\alpha-1}.$$

Using equation (2.17) this becomes

$$\frac{\widehat{r}_t}{1 - \tau_k} + \delta = \alpha * K_t^{\alpha-1}.$$

Thus we can explicitly solve for the per-capita stock of capital, given estimates of $\widehat{r}_t$, δ, and α as

$$K_t = \left[\frac{1}{\alpha} \left(\frac{\widehat{r}_t}{1 - \tau_k} + \delta \right) \right]^{\frac{1}{\alpha-1}} \tag{2.18}$$

We can use (2.18) to solve for K_t in each of the countries. For both countries, set α to 0.32, the annual depreciation rate to 5.5 percent per year ($\delta = 0.055$), and the required after-tax return on capital to 6 percent ($\widehat{r}_t = 0.06$). In the country with the lower tax rate on capital income of 40 percent, the stock of capital is

$$K_t = \left[\frac{1}{0.32} \left(\frac{0.06}{1 - 0.40} + 0.055 \right) \right]^{\frac{1}{0.32-1}} = 2.904.$$

In this country, output is

$$Y_t = K_t^{\alpha} = 2.904^{0.32} = 1.407.$$

Wages paid to labor, $w_t L_t$, are equal to 68 percent of output – see equation (2.11). Given $L_t = 1$, the wage rate (before labor income taxes) is 0.956.

In the country with the higher tax rate on capital income of 60 percent, the stock of capital is

$$K_t = \left[\frac{1}{0.32} \left(\frac{0.06}{1 - 0.60} + 0.055 \right) \right]^{\frac{1}{0.32-1}} = 1.925.$$

In this country, output is

$$Y_t = K_t^\alpha = 1.458^{0.32} = 1.233,$$

and the wage rate before labor income taxes is 0.839.

So the country with the lower capital income tax has (a) 51 percent more capital $(2.904/1.925 - 1)$, (b) 14 percent more output $(1.407/1.233 - 1)$, and (c) a 14 percent higher hourly wage rate $(0.956/0.839 - 1)$ – even though the countries have identical technology levels and identical labor inputs.

It may seem odd to you at first to think that a reduction in the capital income tax rate could benefit workers via an increase in wages. The reason it may seem counter-intuitive is that certain media groups and some politicians emphasize the redistributive nature of capital income taxation. A relatively small segment of the population owns a disproportionate share of the capital stock, and for this reason taxation of capital income seems like a straightforward redistribution of income from wealthy capital owners to workers (i.e. the rest of the population, most of whom work). However, the media and politicians typically fail to mention the implications of capital income taxes on efficiency and productivity. According to our production function, labor needs capital to be effective. And higher capital income tax rates discourage the accumulation of capital, which leads to lower output and lower wages. When viewed in this light, a higher rate of taxation on capital income tends to make workers worse off. This logic explains why many economists, including some left of center politically, argue for reducing the tax rate on capital income.

This example also illustrates why China and other developing countries might never truly catch up to the US, meaning their per-capita real GDP and hourly real wage rates may not ever match those of the US. The stories of corruption, cronyism, bribes, and such, if true, suggest that the implicit tax rate on capital income in rapidly developing countries may be quite high. And, as our simple example shows, when tax rates on capital income are relatively high, the levels of capital, output, and wages are relatively low.

2.4 Measurement of K_t, L_t, and z_t

2.4.1 Measurement of the Capital Stock

Recall that the capital stock in period $t + 1$, K_{t+1}, is a function of the capital stock in period t (K_t) less some depreciation, denoted δK_t, plus any new investment that occurs, denoted I_t:

$$K_{t+1} = K_t - \delta K_t + I_t$$

$$= K_t (1 - \delta) + I_t. \tag{2.19}$$

The same relationship also held in period t,

$$K_t = K_{t-1} (1 - \delta) + I_{t-1}. \tag{2.20}$$

Substituting equation (2.20) into (2.19) and rearranging terms yields

$$K_{t+1} = I_t + (1 - \delta) I_{t-1} + K_{t-1}(1 - \delta)^2.$$

Now, if we repeat this substitution, but for K_{t-1}, K_{t-2}, and so forth, we eventually wind up with the following identity:

$$K_{t+1} = I_t + (1 - \delta) I_{t-1} + (1 - \delta)^2 I_{t-2}$$

$$+ (1 - \delta)^3 I_{t-3} + \cdots \tag{2.21}$$

$$= \sum_{s=0}^{\infty} (1 - \delta)^s I_{t-s}. \tag{2.22}$$

That is, the capital stock is the sum of all past investment decisions, after appropriately accounting for the fact that capital depreciates.

Equation (2.21) (or 2.22) is called a "perpetual inventory" accounting equation, and the BEA uses this accounting to estimate capital stocks in the United States. The BEA's estimates of the capital stock are available on the BEA's webpage. Go to the BEA's home page at www.bea.gov, click on the "Fixed Assets" link, then click on the "Interactive Tables: Fixed Assets Tables" link, and then click on the "Standard Fixed Assets Tables" link. The nominal estimates of the entire stock of capital are available in Table 1.1 (see Figure 2.1). The estimates of the real stock can be derived from the data in Table 1.2 (not shown).[8]

We can use data from the BEA to compute the ratio of the capital stock to annual output for 2006. First, go to Fixed Assets Table 1.1 and mark down nominal "current-cost" total private fixed assets not including the stock of consumer durable goods, line 2, as $31,818.5 billion. Add to this nominal state and local government fixed assets, $6,909.4[9] and nominal federal government non-defense assets[10] of $708.7 billion; these estimates are available in Fixed Assets Table 7.1 (not shown). From this, subtract line 7 of Fixed Assets Table 1.1, nominal private residential fixed assets ($17,103.5), under the assumption that residential structures (i.e. housing structures) do not directly contribute to the capital stock used to produce GDP.[11]

---

[8] Real stocks are not directly reported in table 1.2, but quantity indexes are reported. To convert the quantity indexes into real stocks in constant $2000, multiply the quantity indexes that are reported in this table by the nominal value of each of the stocks in 2000 that are reported in Table 1.1 and then divide each by 100.

[9] These are largely schools and roads, which we assume to add to the productive capacity of the US economy.

[10] Of course federal defense is important, but the stock of federal defense capital may not directly produce measured GDP.

[11] One exception is the category of consumption called "consumption of housing services," discussed next.

	Bureau of Economic Analysis Fixed Asset Table	
	Table 1.1. Current-Cost Net Stock of Fixed Assets and Consumer Durable Goods [Billions of dollars; yearend estimates] Today is: 6/24/2008 Last Revised on August 08, 2007	
Line		**2006**
1	**Fixed assets and consumer durable goods**	**44,432.0**
2	**Fixed assets**	**40,556.9**
3	Private	31,818.5
4	Nonresidential	14,715.0
5	Equipment and software	5,027.9
6	Structures	9,687.1
7	Residential	17,103.5
8	Government	8,738.5
9	Nonresidential	8,397.1
10	Equipment and software	856.6
11	Structures	7,540.6
12	Residential	341.4
13	**Consumer durable goods**	**3,875.1**
	Addenda:	
14	**Private and government fixed assets**	**40,556.9**
15	Nonresidential	23,112.1
16	Equipment and software	5,884.4
17	Structures	17,227.6
18	Residential	17,444.9
19	**Government fixed assets**	**8,738.5**
20	Federal	1,829.0
21	State and local	6,909.4

Figure 2.1 Bureau of Economic Analysis Fixed Asset Table 1.1: Current-cost net stock of fixed assets and consumer durable goods

After these calculations, we estimate the nominal stock of non-defense US capital used in the production of GDP in 2006 to have been $22,333.1.

Now, turn to NIPA Table 1.1.5 (see Figure 2.2). Annual nominal GDP in 2006 was $13,194.7, line 1. From this, subtract the only component of GDP that is directly derived from the stock of residential assets: "consumption of housing services," which in 2006 is estimated to have been (in nominal terms) $1,381.3 for the year – see line 14 of NIPA Table 2.3.5 (see Figure 2.3). This correction aligns our capital measure more closely with our measure of output. After this adjustment, we estimate annual nominal GDP less the nominal consumption of housing services in 2006 to have been $11,813.4.

Bureau of Economic Analysis
National Income and Product Accounts Table

Table 1.1.5. Gross Domestic Product
[Billions of dollars]

Today is: 6/24/2008   Last Revised on May 29, 2008   Next Release Date June 26, 2008

Line		2006
1	**Gross domestic product**	**13,194.7**
2	**Personal consumption expenditures**	**9,224.5**
3	Durable goods	1,048.9
4	Nondurable goods	2,688.0
5	Services	5,487.6
6	**Gross private domestic investment**	**2,209.2**
7	Fixed investment	2,162.5
8	Nonresidential	1,397.7
9	Structures	405.1
10	Equipment and software	992.6
11	Residential	764.8
12	Change in private inventories	46.7
13	**Net exports of goods and services**	**-762.0**
14	Exports	1,467.6
15	Goods	1,030.5
16	Services	437.1
17	Imports	2,229.6
18	Goods	1,880.4
19	Services	349.2
20	**Government consumption expenditures and gross investment**	**2,523.0**
21	Federal	932.5
22	National defense	624.3
23	Nondefense	308.2
24	State and local	1,590.5

Figure 2.2 Bureau of Economic Analysis National Income and Product Accounts Table 1.1.5: Gross domestic product

Putting these calculations together, our estimate of the nominal stock of capital to nominal annual output in the US in 2006 is $1.89 = \$22,333.1/\$11,813.4$. Different economists have estimated different ratios for K/Y and estimates differ depending on what is explicitly included or excluded from either capital or GDP. As noted earlier, if the price of investment, consumption, and output coincide (which would occur if consumption and investment goods were produced using the same production function) then the ratio of nominal

Bureau of Economic Analysis
National Income and Product Accounts Table

Table 2.3.5. Personal Consumption Expenditures by Major Type of Product
[Billions of dollars]

Today is: 6/24/2008   Last Revised on May 29, 2008   Next Release Date June 26, 2008

Line		2006
1	**Personal consumption expenditures**	**9,224.5**
2	**Durable goods**	**1,048.9**
3	Motor vehicles and parts	434.2
4	Furniture and household equipment	404.1
5	Other	210.6
6	**Nondurable goods**	**2,688.0**
7	Food	1,259.3
8	Clothing and shoes	357.2
9	Gasoline, fuel oil, and other energy goods	340.1
10	Gasoline and oil	318.6
11	Fuel oil and coal	21.6
12	Other	731.4
13	**Services**	**5,487.6**
14	Housing	1,381.3
15	Household operation	501.6
16	Electricity and gas	209.8
17	Other household operation	291.8
18	Transportation	340.6
19	Medical care	1,587.7
20	Recreation	381.0
21	Other	1,295.3
	Addenda:	
22	Energy goods and services [1]	550.0
23	Personal consumption expenditures excluding food and energy	7,415.3

Figure 2.3 Bureau of Economic Analysis National Income and Product Accounts Table 2.3.5: Personal consumption expenditures by major type of product

capital to nominal output will be the same as the ratio of real capital to real output.[12]

Using the method we have just described to compute the nominal capital-output ratio for earlier years, Figure 2.4 plots estimates of this ratio over the 1929-2006 period. On average, the ratio of capital to annual output has been about 1.8. Starting from 1950, the capital-output ratio has remained stable and near its trend average. One of the reasons economists write that the US has been on a balanced-growth

---

[12] The nominal capital-output ratio will not be the same as the real capital-output ratio when capital goods are produced using a different technology than all other goods and services in the economy. Extensions of the model of firms presented in this chapter allow investment goods and other components of GDP to be produced using different technologies.

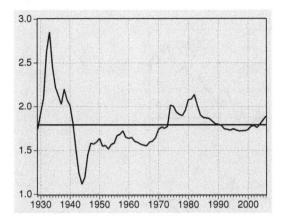

Figure 2.4 The ratio of the nominal value of capital to nominal annual output, 1929–2006

path since 1950 is that the capital-output ratio has not moved too far away from its average over the 1950–2006 period.

Given our measurement of the stock of capital, we can use other BEA data to estimate the annual depreciation rate on the stock of capital. Estimates of the annual nominal dollar value of depreciated capital are reported in Fixed Assets Tables 1.3 and 7.3 (the analog to Fixed Assets Tables 1.1 and 7.1, but for depreciation) (not shown). Taking the nominal stock of capital as we have defined it as given, the average annual rate of depreciation over the 1930–2006 period, shown in Figure 2.5, is 5.4 percent. In each period we compute the effective rate of depreciation as the dollar value of depreciated capital during year t divided by the nominal value of the capital stock as of year-end in year $t - 1$.[13] As is obvious from Figure 2.5, the annual depreciation rate on the stock of capital has been increasing over time for a variety of reasons we will not discuss in this book; by the

[13] Technical note: the BEA's reported capital stock for any year t is for year-end (Dec. 31) of year t.

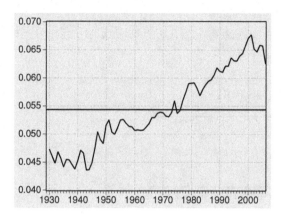

Figure 2.5 The depreciation rate of capital, δ, 1930–2006

end of the sample, the annual depreciation rate on capital is around 6.3 percent.

We can use our estimates of the average capital-output ratio and depreciation rates to guess an economy-wide average rate of taxation on capital income. Recall from equation (2.9) that optimizing firms set the pre-tax marginal product of capital equal to

$$r_t = \alpha \left(\frac{Y_t}{K_t} \right). \tag{2.23}$$

Given an estimate of α of 0.32 and an estimate of the ratio of capital to annual output of 1.8 (which implies an annual output-capital ratio of $1/1.8 = 0.556$), we estimate the marginal product of capital in the US on average in 1929–2006 to have been

$$r_t = 0.32 * 0.556 = 0.178, \tag{2.24}$$

about 18 percent per year.

Now rewrite equation (2.17), the expression linking depreciation rates, tax rates, and the marginal product of capital to after-tax returns, as

Table 2.3 **Effective tax rates (%), 1996, G7 countries**			
Country*	Capital income	Labor income	Consumption
Canada	50.66	32.63	10.37
France	26.11	50.08	15.97
Germany	23.91	42.38	16.40
Italy	33.86	49.77	14.72
Japan	42.61	27.44	6.00
United Kingdom	47.17	24.41	15.25
United States	39.62	27.73	5.47

* These estimates are taken from Professor Enrique Mendoza's website, www.econ.umd.edu/~mendoza/pp/newtaxdata.pdf.

$$\tau_k = 1 - \frac{\widehat{r}_t}{r_t - \delta}. \tag{2.25}$$

Suppose the worldwide return on capital, net of taxes and depreciation is 6 percent, $\widehat{r}_t = 0.06$. Using $r = 0.178$ and an estimate of $\delta = 0.054$, we estimate the tax rate on capital income in the U.S., over the 1929–2006 period, to be

$$\tau_k = 1 - \frac{0.06}{0.178 - 0.054} = 0.515. \tag{2.26}$$

Intuitively this tax rate seems very high, but a standard estimate of the tax rate on capital income in the US is about 40 percent. The United States has about the median tax rate on capital income of all the G7 countries, shown in Table 2.3. In contrast, taxes on labor income and on consumption in the United States are low relative to the other G7 countries.[14]

---

[14] The estimates shown in Table 2.3 are computed using the procedure described in E. Mendoza, A. Razin, and L. Tesar, 1994, "Effective Tax Rates in Macroeconomics. Cross-country Estimates of Tax Rates on Factor Income and Consumption," *Journal of Monetary Economics*, vol. 34, pp. 297–323.

2.4.2 Measurement of the Labor Input

We will measure annual hours worked – that is, the labor input L_t – as the sum of the hours worked in the marketplace of all workers in the economy during the year.[15] Of course, this raises two issues.

1. How do we actually measure hours worked?

    The BLS measures hours worked in the United States using two surveys: a monthly payroll survey and a survey of households. The payroll survey is a survey of hours worked at 390,000 big firms who employ roughly 47 million non-farm wage and salary workers, full- or part-time, who receive pay during the payroll period. The household survey is a survey of the hours worked from a randomly selected group of 50,000 households in 792 sample areas that are chosen to represent all counties and independent cities in the US. An advantage of the household survey is that, since it is random, it covers hours worked from both big and small firms. A disadvantage is that the sample size is small.

    Besides sample size and coverage issues, there are other important differences between the surveys; a summary of these differences can be found at the BLS website: www.bls.gov/ lau/lauhvse.htm. There used to be (and may still be) some debate about which survey yielded a more accurate snapshot of the labor input. I think most economists view changes to the payroll survey as more indicative of changes to the labor input than changes to the household survey. For example, Alan Greenspan (former chairman of the Board of Governors of the Federal Reserve) weighed in on this issue in his testimony to Congress on February 11, 2004: "I wish I could say the household survey were the more accurate.

---

[15] We exclude all non-market hours of work, such as cleaning, cooking, and child-care done at home.

Everything we've looked at suggests that it's the payroll data which are the series which you have to follow."

2. Should we quality-adjust hours we measure? That is, should we treat all hours from all workers as identical?

Many economists, when thinking about the aggregate labor input, do not quality-adjust hours – they just add up all the hours worked in the market by all people that work. This is (almost) certainly a mistake in the sense that some people are more productive with the same set of tools than other people. However, a case can be made that perhaps it is sometimes inappropriate to quality-adjust hours. In many of the models macroeconomists write to study the macroeconomy, all people are treated as identical. It can therefore be argued that the raw hours data should not be adjusted if the treatment of the data is to be completely consistent with the assumptions of the models.

The BEA reports (the BLS) estimates of the aggregate hours input for the US economy in NIPA Table 6.9. Figure 2.6 graphs the ratio of hours worked per week from the NIPA (annual hours worked by domestic employees divided by 52) to the civilian non-institutionalized population aged 16 and older.[16] This graph shows that people have spent an average of 19.5 hours per week at work since World War II. The reason the average per-capita hours worked each week is not 35 or 40, as you might have expected, is that (a) many potential workers are in school aged 16–25, (b) many women and men aged 25–50 do not work in the market but work at home taking care of children,[17] and (c) retirees do not work at all.

---

[16] The population data come from the BLS website, ftp://ftp.bls.gov/pub/special.requests/lf/aat1.txt. The data in NIPA Table 6.9 begin in 1949, explaining the sample range of Figure 2.6.

[17] As mentioned, this kind of work is not counted in the national employment statistics.

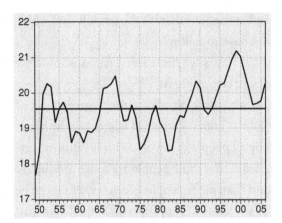

Figure 2.6 Per-capita hours worked per week, 1949–2006

The graph suggests that per-capita time spent working has been roughly trendless since World War II, and other evidence suggests it may have been trendless for over a century.[18] The fact that real wages have been rising (making the price of leisure more expensive, as we will discuss in Chapter 3) and hours worked per week have been trendless has implications for how economists model the utility households receive from leisure.

As you can also see from Figure 2.6, the per-capita labor input fluctuates around its fairly constant trend. Labor economists study the volatility of the labor input using three concepts: the labor force, the labor force participation rate, and the unemployment rate.

- The BLS defines the labor force as follows:[19] All members of the civilian non-institutional population are eligible for inclusion in the labor force, and those 16 and over who have a job or are actively looking for one are so classified. All others – those who

---

[18] See V. Ramey and N. Francis, 2009, "A Century of Work and Leisure," *American Economic Journal: Macroeconomics*, forthcoming.

[19] This definition is taken from www.bls.gov/cps/cps_faq.htm#Ques4.

have no job and are not looking for one – are counted as "not in the labor force." Many who do not participate in the labor force are going to school or are retired. Family responsibilities keep others out of the labor force. Still others have a physical or mental disability which prevents them from participating in labor force activities.

- The labor force participation rate is defined as the labor force (the sum of employed and unemployed workers) divided by the number of potential workers, typically the non-institutionalized population aged 16–65 excluding students and homemakers. In May, 2008 the US labor force participation rate was estimated to have been 66.2 percent.

- The unemployment rate is the percentage of individuals that are unemployed and actively looking for a job divided by the labor force.[20] As of May, 2008 the US unemployment rate was estimated to have been 5.5 percent.

Data on the unemployment rate, the participation rate, and the work force is collected by the BLS. To access this data, go to the BLS website www.bls.gov and click on the "National Unemployment Rate" link, which will lead you to www.bls.gov/cps/home.htm. A nice one-page summary of the annual data is directly available here: ftp:// ftp.bls.gov/pub/special.requests/lf/aat1.txt.

I will not have much of any interest to say about why the unemployment rate fluctuates. One reason is that research-oriented macroeconomists are only beginning to integrate labor market models of search and matching frictions between employees and employers – models that naturally lead to unemployment as a distinct and necessary state of the world – with more traditional models of consumption

---

[20] A person without a job who is not actively seeking employment is called "discouraged" and is not called "unemployed."

and investment.[21] In many models, macroeconomists assume households optimally choose to adjust – up or down – their labor supply
in response to cyclical wages. Although this has intuitive appeal in
certain situations – for example, teenagers and retirees can enter and
leave the work force depending on current market wages – it is not
that useful a framework for modeling involuntary layoffs in the midst
of a recession.

2.4.3 Measurement of Technology

Given estimates of the real capital stock, hours worked in production
and real output, measurement of technology is straightforward. Recall
from earlier in this chapter that the natural logarithm of the Cobb–
Douglas production function has the following expression

$$\ln(Y_t) = \ln(z_t) + \alpha \ln(K_t) + (1 - \alpha) \ln(L_t).$$

Given data on real output, the real stock of capital, and hours worked,
and given an estimate of $\alpha = 0.32$, we can solve for the natural log of
technology, $\ln(z_t)$, as

$$\ln(z_t) \equiv \ln(Y_t) - \alpha \ln(K_t) - (1 - \alpha) \ln(L_t).$$

For labor hours L_t, we use data on hours worked by full-time
and part-time domestic employees from NIPA Table 6.9. For the
real capital stock, we add together the real stock of non-residential
private fixed assets from Fixed Assets Table 1.2 and the real stocks of

---

[21] Three important recent papers on this topic are D. Andolfatto, 1996, "Business
Cycles and Labor-Market Search," *American Economic Review*, vol. 86,
pp. 112–132; R. Shimer, 2005, "The Cyclical Behavior of Equilibrium
Unemployment and Vacancies," *American Economic Review*, vol. 95, pp. 25–49;
and M. Hagedorn, and I. Manovskii, 2008, "The Cyclical Behavior of Equilibrium
Unemployment and Vacancies Revisited," *American Economic Review*, vol. 98, pp.
1692–1706.

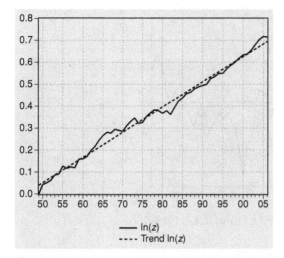

Figure 2.7 $\ln(z_t)$ and its trend, with $\ln(z_t)$ rescaled to 0.0 in 1949, 1949–2006

federal non-defense capital and all state and local capital from Fixed Assets Table 7.2.[22] For real output, we subtract the real consumption of housing services (NIPA Table 2.3.3) from real GDP (NIPA Table 2.3.3). Note we use real, and not nominal, data on output and capital stocks. Otherwise – and this is unlike our estimates of the capital-output ratio and depreciation rate – our estimates of changes to z_t will not be accurate: They will be contaminated by changes to the inflation rate.

The solid line in Figure 2.7 is our estimate of the natural logarithm of z_t. The dotted line in this figure shows the path of the natural logarithm of z_t if z_t had increased at a constant and fixed growth rate over the 1949–2006 time period. The exact value of the natural log of z_t at any particular date is unimportant for the same reason that the level of real GDP is unimportant, so I have taken the liberty of rescaling the natural log of z_t to 0.0 in 1949. By doing this, we can

---

[22] See footnote 8.

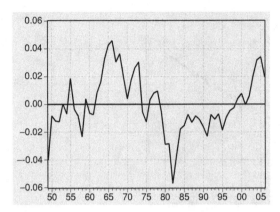

Figure 2.8 Deviations of ln (z_t) from trend, 1949–2006

see directly from the graph that the natural log of z_t has increased by 0.71 units since 1949; this implies that the level of z_t has increased by 2.04 times from 1949 to 2006.

Figure 2.8 plots the deviations of ln (z_t) from its straight-line trend (the dotted line in Figure 2.7) over the 1949–2006 period. It is clear that ln (z_t) does not always exactly follow its trend, but always seems to return to it – in fact, that is the definition of a trend![23] We can use statistical tools to determine the average number of years that z_t tends to stay away from its trend, when it is away from its trend. To do this, we first regress the deviation of ln (z_t) from its trend (see Figure 2.8) on its lagged value. The coefficient from this regression is 0.76. This coefficient tells us that in the absence of all other shocks, next year's value of the deviation of ln (z_{t+1}) from trend will equal 0.76 times this year's value of the deviation of ln (z_t) from trend. A little mathematics shows that the "half-life" of a shock to ln (z_t) is 2.5 years, meaning that absent any other shocks, in 2.5 years the value of the deviation of ln z from trend will be exactly half of the current value

---

[23] We discuss trends and cycles in much more detail in Chapter 5.

of the deviation of ln (z_t) from trend.[24] This means that "technology shocks," loosely defined as deviations of the level of technology away from trend, are long-lived but not permanent. We will use this insight to explain the source of business cycles in Chapter 5.

FURTHER READING

- We have assumed in this chapter that all capital is used in production in every period. Of course, some capital can lie idle at times. Data on the "capacity utilization" of capital is released by the Federal Reserve Board, and these data are available at www. federal-reserve.gov/releases/g17.

- Although we have treated all capital as identical in this chapter, when the BEA constructs capital stocks it aggregates across many different types of capital and allows for a different depreciation rate for each type of capital. A list of depreciation rates by type of capital is available on the BEA website in the article by Barbara Fraumeini, 1997, "The Measurement of Depreciation in the US National Income and Product Accounts," Survey of Current Business, July, available at www.bea.gov/scb/pdf/national/ niparel/1997/0797fr.pdf. The BEA also has another document detailing its construction of capital stocks, "Fixed Assets and Consumer Durable Goods in the United States, 1925–97," published in September, 2003, and available at www.bea.gov/national/pdf/Fixed_Assets_1925_97.pdf.

---

[24] The half-life of a shock is the number of years it takes for the shock to lose half its value. With a regression coefficient of 0.76, the half-life is the value of x such that $0.76^x = 0.5$. x can be solved as $x = \ln(0.5) / \ln(0.76) = 2.53$.

• There is a strand of macroeconomic theory called "endogenous growth" that models growth in technology as the outcome of an investment in research and development programs. Wikipedia has a very brief overview of the theory at http://en.wikipedia.org/wiki/Endogenous_growth_theory. Professor Paul Romer has done some influential work on the topic, and Ronald Bailey at *Reason* magazine has an interesting interview with him in December, 2001, available at www.reason.com/news/show/28243.html.

• Variation in the level of real GDP, in absolute and in per-capita terms, over the 1950–2004 period is available at the Penn World Tables, at http://pwt.econ.upenn.edu/php_site/pwt_index.php. The Penn World Tables use an exchange rate called "purchasing power parity" to convert all country currencies into US dollars. We discuss purchasing power parity in some detail in chapter 4.

Ⓗ Homework

1 Explain why the following thinking – an example of Marx's labor theory of value as written on the website http://isil.org/resources/lit/labor-theory-val.html – does not follow from our model of production:

A worker in a factory is given $30 worth of material, and after working 3 hours producing a good, and using $10 worth of fuel to run a machine, he creates a product which is sold for $100. According to Marx, the labor and only the labor of the worker increased the value of the natural materials to $100. The worker is thus justly entitled to a $60 payment, or $20 per hour.

2 Write down a Cobb–Douglas production function. Show that the marginal product of capital is declining in the amount of capital, and that the marginal product of labor is declining in the amount of labor.

3 Define the average product of labor, or productivity. Why do wages rise with productivity?

4 Write down a Cobb–Douglas production function.

a. What has capital's share of income been over the past 50 years? What parameter of the Cobb–Douglas production function relates to capital's share of income?

b. Referring to the specific elements of the Cobb–Douglas production function, explain why China's GDP has increased so rapidly.

5 Suppose that output in period t is produced according to the following function:

$$Y_t = K_t^\alpha \, (z_t L_t)^{1-\alpha}$$

and suppose that firms pay r_t for each unit of capital and w_t for each unit of labor.

a. Define firm profits.

b. Show that if r_t is constant over time, profit-maximization by firms implies that Y_t and K_t increase at the same rate.

c. Denote the growth rate of Y_t as g_Y, the growth rate of K_t as g_K, the growth rate of L_t as g_L, and the growth rate of z_t as g_z. Assume that r_t is constant over time, and then show why $g_Y = g_z + g_L$.

6 Suppose that in any year t, output (Y_t) is produced according to the following production function:

$$Y_t = z_t^\gamma K_t^\alpha L_t^\beta$$

where z_t is technology, K_t is capital used in production, and L_t is labor used in production. Determine the annual growth rate of Y_t, call it g_Y, as a function of the annual growth rate of technology, g_z, the annual growth rate of capital in production, g_K, and the annual growth rate of labor in production, g_L. Show work.

7 Suppose a representative firm produces output each period according to the Cobb–Douglas production function described in class,

$$Y_t = z_t K_t^\alpha L_t^{1-\alpha}.$$

Holding the labor input constant, why is it that technology growth is required for sustained increases to per-capita real GDP? That is, why is it impossible for a country to sustainably increase real GDP per capita through the accumulation of capital alone?

8 Assume the economy produces output according to the Cobb–Douglas production function

$$Y_t = z_t K_t^\alpha L_t^{1-\alpha}.$$

The economy-wide ratio of capital to output is 2.0. Assume capital share in production is 0.32. What is the pre-tax and pre-depreciation rental rate on a unit of capital? Show work.

9 Assume the following about India: (a) the depreciation rate on capital is 6 percent; (b) capital's share of production is 30 percent; (c) the after-tax and after-depreciation rate of return on capital is

6 percent; and (d) the capital income tax rate (inclusive of bribes and corruption) is 70 percent.

What is the economy-wide ratio of capital to output in India?

10 Consider a Cobb–Douglas production function $Y = zK^\alpha L^{1-\alpha}$ with a capital share of 0.32.

Suppose $z = 2$, $K = 2$ and $L = 2$.

a. What is output?
b. What is productivity?
c. Suppose z doubles to 4, but K and L remain fixed at 2. What are output and productivity now?
d. Suppose K and L double to 4, but z remains fixed at 2. What are output and productivity now?

11 You have been told the following:

- The average product of labor is 2.5614.
- The capital-labor ratio is 2.5.
- The depreciation rate on capital is 10 percent.
- The capital share of production is 0.32.
- The world-wide after-tax rate of return on assets (capital) is 6 percent.

Answer the following:

a. What is the marginal product of labor?
b. What is the marginal product of capital?
c. What is the tax rate on capital income in this economy?

12 Suppose that the ratio of K/Y is roughly constant, and consistent with this suppose that the rate of growth of real output and real capital (not per capita) are 3 percent per year. Finally, suppose that the depreciation rate on capital is 5.5 percent per year.

a. What is the investment-capital ratio, i.e. the ratio of I/K?

b. Suppose the capital-output ratio is 1.8. What is the ratio of I/Y?

c. In the 1973:1 to 2007:4 data, what is the average ratio of the sum of (a) private non-residential fixed investment, (b) federal government non-defense investment, and (c) state and local investment to GDP less the consumption of housing services?

3 | Households and Asset Pricing

O Objectives of this Chapter

In this chapter, we describe how economists model the optimizing behavior of households. Specifically, we study how households decide on the quantity of labor to supply to the market and on the allocation of current income and assets to consumption and savings.

Throughout this chapter we assume that households are identical, implying the study of one "representative" household is equivalent to the study of all households. As with the case of our study of firms in Chapter 2, we make this assumption not because we believe it to be true, but because it enables us to write down a model that we can solve and from which we can derive intuition for how the economy functions. If we were to add more realism, the models would be more difficult to solve, and our intuition on the key economic tradeoffs underlying the decision process might not profoundly change.

We start the chapter by studying the optimal labor supply problem of households. We will assume that households receive utility from two goods, consumption and leisure. The key tradeoff is as follows: if households work additional hours, they have more income to spend on consumption but enjoy less leisure. We show that if households have preferences for leisure N and consumption C of the form $\theta \ln (C) + (1 - \theta) \ln (N)$, and all income is spent on consumption in each period, then optimal labor supply is independent of the after-tax wage. The result that labor supply is independent of wage is consistent with data (from Chapter 2) that suggest aggregate hours worked per week have been trendless since 1949 at about 19.5 hours per week even though real wages have been rising over the 1949–2006 period.

Next, we consider the optimal consumption and savings decision problem of households where households have access to only one type of asset in which they can save. In this segment of the chapter, we will introduce concepts such as time-separable preferences, discounting, time-consistent behavior and rational expectations. We will assume that households receive utility from two goods, consumption today and consumption in the future. We show that the price of consumption today relative to the price of consumption in the future is the interest rate on this asset and thus the optimal household decision on how much to save for future consumption depends on this interest rate. When the interest rate is low, the price of current consumption relative to future consumption is low, and current consumption is relatively high, implying relatively low saving; when the interest rate is high, the price of current consumption relative to future consumption is high, and future consumption is relatively high, implying relatively high saving. We end this segment of the chapter by discussing some of the assumptions about human behavior implied by this model.

Because interest rates are the key price for determining optimal household saving, the theory of household saving naturally leads to a discussion of asset pricing. In the third segment of the chapter, we consider a model where households have the ability to save in more than one type of asset. First, we allow households to simultaneously save in stocks and bonds. We show that our model implies that all assets in the economy must pay the same risk-adjusted return, and the model has a precise definition of risk. When we apply this theory to data, it appears that the premium to a portfolio of stocks over a risk-free asset (such as Treasuries) should be low, about 1 percent. Over the 1929–2007 period, the average yearly premium of stock returns over one-month Treasury Bills has been about 7.5 percent. This discrepancy between model predictions and data has led to an "equity-premium puzzle" in the academic literature, and researchers are actively investigating how models of household consumption and saving behavior need to be adjusted such that the model-predicted premium to stocks over Treasury Bills aligns with the data.

Next, we consider a model in which households can simultaneously save in either a portfolio of financial assets or housing. We show that the risk-adjusted expected return to housing must be the same as the risk-adjusted expected return to financial assets. We document that the return to housing has two pieces, a dividend yield (defined as the ratio of rents to prices, the "rent-price ratio") and a capital gain. We prove that the price of housing is equal to the discounted stream of rental flows, where the discount rate is the return to housing. We then show that when both the return to housing and the growth rate of rents are constants, the growth rate of house prices should equal the growth rate of rents. Finally, we discuss data on rent-price ratios. Specifically, we discuss the fact that rent-price ratios are lower in some cities (such as San Francisco) than in others (such as Houston) and, given these data, we discuss the implications for the expected rate of growth of house prices in those cities. We also discuss changes to the aggregate rent-price ratio over time. We show that the aggregate rent-price ratio fell by a substantial margin (1.5 percentage points) during the 1997–2006 housing boom in the United States. We compare the change in the rent-price ratio to the change in yield on a 10-year Treasury Bond over the same period.

In the final segment of the chapter, we study a unified model of household labor supply and savings. We show that this model does not predict that labor supply is constant, but depends on wages. Finally, in an example of a "calibration" exercise, we use the predictions of the model to estimate the parameter of household utility that determines the utility of consumption received in the future relative to the utility of consumption received today, the so-called "discount factor."

3.1 Optimal Labor Supply with No Saving

In the mathematical appendix, we determine the solution to a house-hold's problem where, given income, a household optimally chooses the quantities of apples and bananas to purchase. The study of labor supply is quite similar, with two exceptions. First, labor supply deter-mines one of the items in the utility function called leisure. Sec-ond, labor supply determines how much income households have to spend.

Instead of apples and bananas, suppose households have prefer-ences for consumption C and leisure N. We're going to define leisure as any time not spent sleeping or engaging in personal care (such as bathing, getting dressed, etc.) less time spent at work. Suppose households have 16 hours a day at their disposal not spent sleeping or attending to personal care. Then, if households work L hours per day, their leisure in hours per day is $N = 16 - L$. We're also going to assume, for simplicity, that each household consists of only one person.

Define household utility for consumption and leisure as follows:

$$\theta \ln(C) + (1 - \theta) \ln(N).$$

Households have two constraints. The first is their time constraint: the sum of hours worked and hours spent enjoying leisure cannot be greater than the time endowment, 16 hours per day. We write this constraint as

$$16 - L - N = 0. \tag{3.1}$$

The second is the budget constraint. We assume that households have no assets and cannot save or borrow, implying household consump-tion must equal after-tax labor income. With these assumptions, the budget constraint linking consumption, labor effort, and income is

$$\widehat{w}L - C = 0. \tag{3.2}$$

$\widehat{w}$ denotes the after-tax wage paid for one hour of labor.

Households in this world have three decisions that are linked: how much to work, how much to consume, and how much leisure to enjoy. It turns out that because households have no savings in this model, these three decisions collapse to only one decision: how many hours to work. Hours of work determines consumption via equation (3.2) and leisure via equation (3.1). Note that we can embed the budget and time constraints directly into the utility function. This gives a utility function that is only a function of L:

$$\theta \ln (\widehat{w}L) + (1 - \theta) \ln (16 - L)$$
$$= \theta \ln (\widehat{w}) + \theta \ln (L) + (1 - \theta) \ln (16 - L).$$

We can maximize this function with respect to L to determine the optimal hours of work. The maximum is achieved when the derivative with respect to L is set equal to zero:

$$\frac{\theta}{L} - \frac{1 - \theta}{16 - L} = 0.$$

Notice that the after-tax wage does not appear anywhere in the equation above. Thus, optimal hours of work,

$$L = \theta * 16,$$

do not depend on the after-tax wage.

Note that we could have proceeded differently to determine the optimal choice of hours worked. It would have been perfectly acceptable to have proceeded in our maximization as if households have three independent decisions, C, L, and N. In this case, we use the Lagrange multiplier technique that is discussed in the appendix to determine the set of choices that maximize the utility of the household. Denote the Lagrange multiplier on the time constraint (3.1) as the Greek letter ξ and the Lagrange multiplier on the budget constraint (3.2) as λ. Then, the Lagrange multiplier technique specifies that household utility is maximized when the derivatives of

$$\theta \ln(C) + (1 - \theta)\ln(N) + \xi\,(16 - L - N) + \lambda\,(\widehat{w}L - C)$$

with respect to the choice variables are equal to zero. That is, to find the allocation of C, N, and L that maximizes household utility, we take the derivative of the above equation three times – once with respect to C, once with respect to N, and and finally with respect to L – and set the derivative equal to zero each time.

When the derivatives with respect to C, N, and L are set to zero, the following equations hold:

$$
\begin{aligned}
C: &\quad \theta/C &= \lambda \\
N: &\quad (1-\theta)/N &= \xi \\
L: &\quad \xi &= \lambda * \widehat{w}.
\end{aligned}
$$

The solution is as follows, which you should prove for homework:

$$
\begin{aligned}
L &= 16 * \theta \\
C &= \widehat{w} * L &= \widehat{w} * 16 * \theta \\
N &= 16 - L &= 16 * (1 - \theta) \\
\lambda &= 1/(\widehat{w} * 16) \\
\xi &= (1/16).
\end{aligned}
$$

Suppose $\theta = 0.174$. Then hours worked per day is $16 * 0.174 = 2.784$, which implies that this household works 19.5 hours per week.

The solution to the particular example implies that the hours worked per day is constant and independent of wages. This means that wages can double and the household will still work 19.5 hours per week. How did this happen? Because of our assumption about the utility of consumption and leisure, it just so happens that income and substitution effects cancel. What does this mean? Suppose that the wage rate increases. Then, holding the labor input constant, households have more income. Because households have more income, they want more consumption and more leisure. Because they desire more leisure, they want to work less. This is called the income effect. However, when the wage rate increases, the price (opportunity cost) of leisure increases. The price of leisure is the wage rate, because each hour of leisure that is taken corresponds to one less hour worked at rate $\widehat{w}$. In most situations, when the price of a good increases, households demand less of that good. So the fact that the price of leisure increases implies that households demand less leisure, and this is called the substitution effect. In this example, the income and substitution effects of the change in wage rates exactly offset, and the amount of labor supplied to the market and the amount of leisure consumed by the household is independent of the wage.

Notice that in this very simple model the government can increase the tax rate on labor, thus reducing the after-tax wage rate, and the supply of labor of $\theta * 16$ hours per day does not change. There was a notion put forth in the late 1970s that labor income taxes in the United States were so high that a reduction in the labor-income tax rate would cause a disproportionate increase in labor supply such that tax revenues would increase. In the example we have just studied, if the government raises the tax rate on wages, tax revenues always increase because the quantity of labor supplied is constant. This does not mean that, in the so-called "real world," labor supply does not respond to the tax rate on labor income. It just means that a prediction about the extent to which labor supply varies with tax rates depends on assumptions about household preferences and constraints.

3.2 Optimal Consumption and Investment

3.2.1 A Two-Period Model

In the previous section, we studied household decision-making assuming that households could not have savings. In the solution, households worked a fixed fraction θ of their discretionary time each period, regardless of the wage. Economists call the model that we solved a "static" model, meaning that in this model households choose variables each period that only affect utility in the current period.

Once we allow households to save, we are considering a "dynamic" model. In a dynamic model, the decisions that a household makes in period t affect its utility in both current and future periods. A model with a savings choice is a dynamic model because households use saving to finance future consumption.

To make this clear, consider a model where households live two periods (young and old, if you like) and receive utility in each period that they are alive from consumption in that period. Define the utility from consumption of C_t in period t as $\ln(C_t)$ and the utility from consumption of C_{t+1} in period $t+1$ as $\ln(C_{t+1})$. In terms of resources, assume the household has some accumulated wealth as of the start of period t. Further, assume (for this section) that the household does not value leisure: it works all the time and receives after-tax labor income in period t of $\widehat{w}_t$ and $\widehat{w}_{t+1}$ in period $t+1$. The question we ask is: how much should the household consume in periods t and $t+1$? If the household consumes as much as possible in period t, then it will have few resources for consumption in $t+1$ and utility will be relatively low in that period.[1] Or, if the household tries to consume as much as possible in $t+1$, then the household will

---

[1] Note that consumption cannot be zero in any period because $\ln(0) = -\infty$.

have little consumption in t and utility in period t will be relatively low in that period.

The household decision-maker will be making decisions in period t that affect both the period t and the period $t + 1$ level of household consumption: consumption in period t determines wealth in period $t + 1$, which determines consumption in period $t + 1$. As long as the household planner is forward-looking, the planner's decision in period t should maximize total remaining lifetime utility. Ignoring the utility value from leisure (for this section of the chapter), remaining lifetime utility of the household, as of period t, has the simple form:

$$\ln{(C_t)} + \beta \ln{(C_{t+1})}, \tag{3.3}$$

where β just weights the utility earned tomorrow, from consuming C_{t+1} tomorrow, to the utility earned today from consuming C_t today. β could be 1.0, but we show at the end of the chapter that β is likely slightly less than 1.0, meaning that, as of today, consumption enjoyed in period $t + 1$ is not quite as valuable to household members, in period t, as consumption enjoyed in period t.

The fact that equation (3.3) looks like the net present value of utility, rather than an expression for current period utility, should not bother you. Equation (3.3) has a different interpretation with which you may be more comfortable. Suppose C_t and C_{t+1} are two different goods, like apples and bananas. Then (3.3) is an expression of today's utility over the two goods and the parameter β weighs the two different goods in today's utility.

The key insight that I will prove to you is that the optimal solution to the household's problem sets the ratio of marginal utilities of these two goods,

$$\left(\frac{1}{C_t} \right) \bigg/ \left(\frac{\beta}{C_{t+1}} \right),$$

equal to the ratio of prices

$$(1 + \widehat{r}_{t+1})/1,$$

where $\widehat{r}_{t+1}$ is the one-period after-tax market rate of return on assets owned at the start of period $t + 1$. $1 + \widehat{r}_{t+1}$ is the price of consumption in period t relative to the price in $t + 1$ because a unit of consumption that is foregone in period t earns $\widehat{r}_{t+1}$ interest.

When we set the ratio of marginal utilities equal to the ratio of prices and rearrange terms, we uncover the relationship:

$$\frac{C_{t+1}}{C_t} = \beta\,(1 + \widehat{r}_{t+1}). \tag{3.4}$$

This equation implies that when after-tax returns on assets are high, people forego some consumption in period t in order to enjoy more consumption in period $t + 1$. When returns on assets are low, people choose to consume in t and enjoy relatively less consumption in period $t + 1$. So, ultimately the rate of return on assets dictates how much people are willing to save to enjoy consumption tomorrow at the expense of consumption today.

3.2.2 Mathematics of the Solution

Before going any further, let's prove that (3.4) holds. As we noted, the household entered period t with a stock of assets from which it can consume. Call these assets A_t. Then assets in period t, income in period t, consumption in period t, and assets in period $t + 1$ (A_{t+1}) are linked according to

$$A_t\,(1 + \widehat{r}_t) + \widehat{w}_t - C_t = A_{t+1}. \tag{3.5}$$

This means that whatever the household does not consume out of assets and income in period t, by definition, must be equal to assets in period $t + 1$. Equation (3.5) is often called an intertemporal budget constraint: it links period t variables, A_t, $\widehat{w}_t$, and C_t, with a period $t + 1$ variable, A_{t+1}.

The same equation holds for period $t + 2$:

$$A_{t+1}(1 + \widehat{r}_{t+1}) + \widehat{w}_{t+1} - C_{t+1} = A_{t+2}. \tag{3.6}$$

If we use equation (3.6) to solve for A_{t+1}, and then substitute this expression for A_{t+1} into equation (3.5), we yield a combined budget constraint of

$$A_t(1 + \widehat{r}_t) + \widehat{w}_t - C_t - \frac{1}{1 + \widehat{r}_{t+1}}[C_{t+1} + A_{t+2} - \widehat{w}_{t+1}] = 0. \tag{3.7}$$

To determine the levels of C_t and C_{t+1} that maximize the utility of the household, we use the Lagrange multiplier technique that is discussed in the appendix. Denote the Lagrange multiplier on the budget constraint (3.7) as λ. Then, the Lagrange multiplier technique specifies that household utility is maximized when the derivatives of

$$\ln(C_t) + \beta \ln(C_{t+1})$$
$$+ \lambda\left(A_t(1 + \widehat{r}_t) + \widehat{w}_t - C_t - \frac{1}{1 + \widehat{r}_{t+1}}[C_{t+1} + A_{t+2} - \widehat{w}_{t+1}]\right) \tag{3.8}$$

with respect to C_t and C_{t+1} are set to zero, which implies:

$$C_t : 1/C_t = \lambda$$
$$C_{t+1} : \beta/C_{t+1} = \lambda/(1 + \widehat{r}_{t+1}).$$

Dividing one equation by the other and rearranging terms yields equation (3.4).

3.2.3 Reinterpreting the Household Budget Constraint

The intertemporal budget constraints (3.5) and (3.6) can be rewritten so that they have the flavor of both NIPA accounting for income and BEA perpetual inventory accounting for wealth. First, recall from section 2.3.4 that the after-tax return on capital is equal to:

$$\widehat{r}_t = (1 - \tau_K) * (r_t - \delta),$$

where τ_K is the tax rate on capital income. Set the tax rate on capital income and labor income to zero for simplicity, so $\widehat{r}_t = (r_t - \delta)$ and $\widehat{w}_t = w_t$. Now, use these definitions to rewrite equation (3.5) as

$$r_t A_t + w_t - C_t + (A_t - \delta A_t - A_{t+1}) = 0. \tag{3.9}$$

Suppose now that there is one representative household in the US economy. This one household's assets is therefore equal to aggregate capital. Replace A everywhere with K in equation (3.9) to yield

$$r_t K_t + w_t - C_t + (K_t - \delta K_t - K_{t+1}) = 0. \tag{3.10}$$

Recall that aggregate investment satisfies the following wealth-accounting equation

$$I_t = K_{t+1} - K_t + \delta K_t,$$

which implies that equation (3.10) can be rewritten as

$$r_t K_t + w_t - C_t - I_t = 0.$$

Finally, $r_t K_t$ is aggregate capital income and w_t (the labor income of this one household) is aggregate labor income. So $r_t K_t + w_t$ is equal to GDP, and thus

$$GDP_t - C_t - I_t = 0.$$

Thus, after abstracting from taxes, government spending, and net exports, the household budget constraint we have considered in our models is consistent with GDP and wealth accounting in the aggregate.

3.2.4 Intertemporal Elasticity of Substitution

The willingness of households to trade off consumption at date t with consumption at date $t+1$ is summarized by a concept called the "intertemporal elasticity of substitution." The elasticity of substitution of any two goods measures the percentage change in the ratio of the quantity consumed of the two consumption goods arising from a 1 percent change in the ratio of marginal utility of those goods. Specifically, if utility is a function of apples (a) and bananas (b), and the marginal utility of apples and bananas is written as MU_a and MU_b, respectively, then the elasticity of substitution of a and b in utility is defined as

$$\frac{\partial \ln (a/b)}{\partial \ln (MU_a/MU_b)}. \tag{3.11}$$

In our model we are concerned with the intertemporal elasticity of substitution because the two goods in utility are consumption at two different periods of time, C_t and C_{t+1}. So, for the two goods in our model, equation (3.11) can be written as

$$\frac{\partial \ln (C_t/C_{t+1})}{\partial \ln (MU_{C_t}/MU_{C_{t+1}})}. \tag{3.12}$$

Recall the utility function of the household is $\ln (C_t) + \beta \ln (C_{t+1})$. The ratio of marginal utilities is

$$\frac{C_{t+1}}{\beta C_t}, \tag{3.13}$$

and the natural log of equation (3.13) is:

$$\ln \left(\frac{C_{t+1}}{C_t} \right) - \ln (\beta)$$

$$= -\ln \left(\frac{C_t}{C_{t+1}} \right) - \ln (\beta).$$

The derivative of this expression with respect to $\ln (C_t/C_{t+1})$ is -1. Thus, with the utility function we are using,

$$\frac{\partial \ln \left(MU_{C_t}/MU_{C_{t+1}} \right)}{\partial \ln (C_t/C_{t+1})} = -1. \tag{3.14}$$

Note that equation (3.14) is the inverse of the elasticity of substitution as defined in equation (3.12). The inverse of -1 is -1, and thus the intertemporal elasticity of substitution between consumption at t and consumption at $t + 1$ is -1.

A more general utility function that is commonly used by macro-economists expresses the utility of consumption at t and at $t + 1$ as

$$\frac{C_t^{1-\sigma}}{1 - \sigma} + \beta \frac{C_{t+1}^{1-\sigma}}{1 - \sigma}, \tag{3.15}$$

where σ is a parameter that is at least 1.0. When σ is exactly equal to 1.0, $C_t^{1-\sigma}/(1 - \sigma)$ yields the same allocations as $\ln (C_t)$.[2] Thus the utility function we have been working with so far in this section is the specific case of equation (3.15) for $\sigma = 1$. Working with utility

---

[2] If we were to subtract a constant value of $1/(1 - \sigma)$ from the utility of consumption in period t – which is not a problem for us because it will not change any allocations – then we can apply L'Hôpital's rule to determine the limit of the utility function as σ approaches 1. That is

$$\lim_{\sigma \to 1} \frac{C_t^{1-\sigma} - 1}{1 - \sigma} = \lim_{\sigma \to 1} \frac{\frac{\partial}{\partial \sigma} \left(C_t^{1-\sigma} - 1 \right)}{\frac{\partial}{\partial \sigma} (1 - \sigma)} = \frac{-1 \ln (C_t)}{-1} = \ln (C_t).$$

The expression in the numerator occurs because $C_t^{1-\sigma}$ can be expressed as $e^{(1-\sigma)\ln(C_t)}$, and the derivative of e^{xa} with respect to x is ae^{ax}.

of C_t and C_{t+1} as stated in equation (3.15), marginal utility at time t divided by the marginal utility at time $t + 1$ is

$$\left(\frac{1}{\beta}\right)\left(\frac{C_t}{C_{t+1}}\right)^{-\sigma} \tag{3.16}$$

The natural log of this expression is

$$-\sigma \ln\left(\frac{C_t}{C_{t+1}}\right) - \ln(\beta). \tag{3.17}$$

The derivative of this expression with respect to $\ln(C_t/C_{t+1})$ is $-\sigma$. Thus, the intertemporal elasticity of substitution for utility as specified in (3.15) is equal to the inverse, $-1/\sigma$. We will use this result later in the chapter.

3.2.5 Discussion of Assumptions

We have made a lot of assumptions in specifying and solving this two-period model. The important assumptions are:

- As of period t, the household cares about consumption in period t and consumption in period $t + 1$.

  A certain fraction of households appears not to save any income at all, or to save very little. There is some debate among economists as to whether these households have "time-inconsistent" preferences, meaning that these households may discount utility from future consumption at a rate that is too high when making their period t consumption decisions, and in such a way that leads to regret once the future arrives. Other economists look at the same evidence and are skeptical; these economists write down models where forward-looking and time-consistent households, under the right circumstances, optimally choose to have little or no savings.

- The household is forward-looking, and knows via the intertemporal budget constraint how consumption in t affects consumption possibilities in $t + 1$.

   This is one facet of the embedded assumption of "rational expectations": the household knows exactly how current consumption affects future consumption possibilities, and acts accordingly. The assumption of rational expectations is relatively new in the field of macroeconomics,[3] but now it is assumed in almost all papers. One reason that the idea of rational expectations has taken hold among macroeconomists is that it is precise. To explain: there is only one way for a household to have rational expectations, and there are an infinite number of ways in which expectations are not rational. So choosing a particular way in which households are not rational is just as arbitrary and perhaps more unappealing than saying that households have rational expectations.

The less important assumptions are:

- The household members only live two periods.

   This assumption is unimportant because the optimal relationship of consumption at $t + 1$ relative to consumption at t, as expressed in equation (3.4), does not change if we assume that the household lives for more than two periods.
- The household members know the interest rate for certain that will prevail in period $t + 1$ as of period t.

   This is not unimportant. With some uncertainty about the future, then the household maximizes expected utility. When there is any uncertainty about future outcomes, equation (3.4) is rewritten to

---

[3] The notion of rational expectations was made famous in a paper by R. Lucas and L. Rapping, 1969, "Real Wages, Employment, and Inflation," *Journal of Political Economy*, vol. 77, pp. 721–754.

allow for this uncertainty as

$$1 = E_t \left[\beta * (C_t / C_{t+1}) * (1 + \widehat{r}_{t+1}) \right], \tag{3.18}$$

where E_t is an expectations operator. Intuitively, equation (3.18) says the following: households may not exactly know the period $t + 1$ after-tax return on capital that will prevail, and, come period $t + 1$ (in response to unforeseen shocks) a household may change its mind about what optimal period $t + 1$ consumption C_{t+1} should be. But equation (3.4) should be expected to hold when a household averages through all the possibilities for period $t + 1$ outcomes in making its decisions in period t, discussed in the next section.

3.2.6 Discussion of Uncertainty

To explain why equation (3.18) holds requires some background on the definition of the expectations operator, E_t. Suppose that a variable x can assume one of $i = 1, \ldots, N$ values. Denote the probability that x_i occurs as ρ_i. Since there are only N different realizations of x, it must be the case that

$$\sum_{i=1}^{N} \rho_i = 1.0.$$

The expected value of x, denoted $E[x]$, is defined as

$$E[x] = \sum_{i=1}^{N} \rho_i x_i.$$

This is the average of the values of x we would observe if we were to draw many realizations of x.

Now consider the case where the probabilities over the different realizations of x can change over time. Denote the probabilities over x in effect at the time in which the expectation is taken, call it date t, as $\rho_{t,i}$. In this case, we denote the expected value of x, given the probabilities over x taken at date t as

$$E_t[x] = \sum_{i=1}^{N} \rho_{t,i} x_i.$$

Let's return to the problem of the optimal savings and consumption decisions of households. Suppose that after-tax labor income and the after-tax rate of return on assets are random in period $t+1$; specifically, suppose there are N possible "states of the world" in period $t+1$, and after-tax income and the after-tax rate of return on assets are potentially different in each state of the world. Label after-tax income and the after-tax rate of return on assets in state i, for $i = 1, \ldots, N$, as $\hat{w}_{t+1,i}$ and $\hat{r}_{t+1,i}$. As before, label the probabilities that state i occurs in $t+1$ (as of time t) as $\rho_{t,i}$.

Given the budget constraint in $t+1$ depends on the realized state of the world in $t+1$, optimal consumption chosen in $t+1$ may depend on the state. Denote consumption chosen in $t+1$ if state i occurs, for $i = 1, \ldots, N$ as $C_{t+1,i}$. If state i occurs, the budget constraint in $t+1$ will be:

$$A_{t+1}\left(1 + \hat{r}_{t+1,i}\right) + \hat{w}_{t+1,i} - C_{t+1,i} = A_{t+2,i} \tag{3.19}$$

In period t it is not know which of the N states of the world will prevail in period $t+1$. Yet households must still make consumption and savings decisions in period t. These savings decisions will determine consumption possibilities in period $t+1$.

To proceed, we assume that households maximize the expected value of utility. That is, we assume that as of time t, households maximize

$$\ln(C_t) + \beta \sum_{i=1}^{N} \rho_{t,i} \ln\left(C_{t+1,i}\right).$$

Notice that this equation is quite similar to equation (3.3), except the certain utility from consumption at period $t+1$ of equation (3.3) is replaced with the expected utility of consumption – the average of the utility from consumption that would occur if we were to repeat period $t + 1$ many times, and in each time draw from the period $t + 1$ distribution of states of the world for after-tax income and return on assets.

A different interpretation of this utility function is that households have utility over $N + 1$ consumption goods: one consumption good (for period t) and N consumption goods for period $t + 1$. In this interpretation, consumption in period $t + 1$ if state i occurs is a different "good" than consumption in period $t + 1$ if state j occurs. The utility weights defining preferences over the N period $t + 1$ consumption goods are given by the probabilities $\rho_{t,i}$ for $i = 1, \ldots, N$.

Under this convenient interpretation, it is as if there are $N + 1$ budget constraints. The first budget constraint is for period t, and it is identical to equation (3.5) from before:

$$A_t (1 + \widehat{r}_t) + \widehat{w}_t - C_t = A_{t+1}. \tag{3.20}$$

The second set of budget constraints are the state-contingent budget constraints listed in equation (3.19). Since there are N possible states in period $t + 1$, there are N possible budget constraints at period $t + 1$, one for each state. To determine optimal consumption C_t and assets to carry forward to period $t + 1$, we set up the Lagrangian for this problem, which has the form:

$$\ln (C_t) + \beta \sum_{i=1}^{N} \rho_{t,i} \ln (C_{t+1,i})$$
$$+ \lambda [A_t (1 + \widehat{r}_t) + \widehat{w}_t - C_t - A_{t+1}]$$
$$+ \sum_{i=1}^{N} \xi_i [A_{t+1} (1 + \widehat{r}_{t+1,i}) + \widehat{w}_{t+1,i} - C_{t+1,i} - A_{t+2,i}]$$

$$\tag{3.21}$$

where λ is the Lagrange multiplier on the period t budget constraint (as before) and ξ_i is the Lagrange multiplier on the period $t + 1$ budget constraint appropriate for state i. There are N possible realizations of the budget constraint and thus N possible period-$t+1$ Lagrange multipliers.

To find the allocation that maximizes household utility, we take derivatives of (3.21) with respect to each of the choice variables and set each derivative to zero:

$$C_t: \qquad 1/C_t = \lambda$$
$$C_{t+1,i}: \beta\rho_{t,i}/C_{t+1,i} = \xi_i \text{ for } i = 1, \ldots, N.$$
$$A_{t+1}: \qquad \lambda = \sum_{i=1}^{N} \xi_i \left(1 + \widehat{r}_{t+1,i}\right).$$

Inserting the first two equations into the third equation and then rearranging terms yields

$$\frac{1}{C_t} = \sum_{i=1}^{N} \frac{\beta\rho_{t,i}}{C_{t+1,i}} \left(1 + \widehat{r}_{t+1,i}\right)$$

$$1 = \sum_{i=1}^{N} \rho_{t,i} \left[\beta \frac{C_t}{C_{t+1,i}} \left(1 + \widehat{r}_{t+1,i}\right)\right]$$

$$\implies 1 = E_t \left[\beta \frac{C_t}{C_{t+1}} \left(1 + \widehat{r}_{t+1}\right)\right].$$

The last equation follows from the definition of the expectations operator.

3.3 Saving and Investment in Multiple Assets

3.3.1 Stocks and Bonds: The Equity Premium Puzzle

Equation (3.18) naturally leads us into a discussion of asset pricing and returns to assets when households have the option of investing in more than one type of asset. Those of you with more of a finance background may have seen a version of equation (3.18) before: In finance, it has the representation of

$$1 = E_t \left[m_{t+1} R_{t+1} \right],$$ (3.22)

where $m_{t+1} = \beta * (C_t / C_{t+1})$ and $R_{t+1} = 1 + \widehat{r}_t$. m_{t+1} is sometimes called a "pricing kernel."

We will show that equation (3.22) should hold for all assets that a household can purchase. Suppose, for example, that equation (3.22) holds for stocks, but not for Treasury Bills. Then no one would invest in Treasury Bills because the return is (say) too low relative to the return on stocks. However, since we observe households investing in both Treasury Bills and stocks, it must be the case that (3.22) simultaneously holds for both stocks and Treasuries.

Denote R_{t+1}^s as equal to $1 + \widehat{r}_t$ for stocks and R_{t+1}^b as equal to $1 + \widehat{r}_t$ for Treasuries. If (3.22) simultaneously holds for stocks and Treasuries, then

$$1 = E_t \left[\beta \left(C_t / C_{t+1} \right) * R_{t+1}^s \right]$$

$$1 = E_t \left[\beta \left(C_t / C_{t+1} \right) * R_{t+1}^b \right]$$

$$\rightarrow 0 = E_t \left[\left(C_t / C_{t+1} \right) * \left(R_{t+1}^s - R_{t+1}^b \right) \right].$$ (3.23)

We subtract the second equation from the first to get the third equation. The variable β drops out because we have divided both the left-hand side and right-hand side by β, and $0/\beta = 0$.

To validate that this equation holds, we will solve the same consumption-saving model as before, but allow households to hold wealth in two types of assets: stocks and Treasury Bills. Denote the value of stocks owned at the start of period $t + 1$ as A_{t+1}^s and the value of Treasury Bills owned at the start of period $t + 1$ as A_{t+1}^b. In period $t + 1$, the budget constraint of the household is

$$0 = A_{t+1}^s R_{t+1}^s + A_{t+1}^b R_{t+1}^b + \widehat{w}_{t+1} - C_{t+1} - A_{t+2}^s - A_{t+2}^b.$$

$$(3.24)$$

As mentioned, R_{t+1}^s is equal to 1 plus the after-tax return on stocks in period $t + 1$ and R_{t+1}^b is equal to 1 plus the after-tax return to Treasury Bills in period $t + 1$. The budget constraint of the household in period t is

$$0 = A_t^s R_t^s + A_t^b R_t^b + \widehat{w}_t - C_t - A_{t+1}^s - A_{t+1}^b. \qquad (3.25)$$

Unlike earlier in the chapter, we will not substitute equation (3.24) into equation (3.25). Rather, since both of these budget constraints will hold, we will assign to each budget constraint its own Lagrange multiplier: we will call the Lagrange multiplier on the period t budget constraint as λ_t and the Lagrange multiplier on the period $t + 1$ budget constraint λ_{t+1}. The fact that the Greek letter λ is the same does not mean that the Lagrange multipliers are identical; rather, they are different variables since λ_t does not have to be equal to λ_{t+1}.

Given a period t wealth endowment of A_t^s and A_t^b (which are not choices in period t), households choose C_t, C_{t+1}, A_{t+1}^s and A_{t+1}^b to maximize $\ln(C_t) + \beta \ln(C_{t+1})$ subject to the two budget constraints given in equations (3.24) and (3.25). The Lagrangian of this problem is

$$
\begin{aligned}
\ln(C_t) &+ \beta \ln(C_{t+1}) \\
&+ \lambda_t \left[A_t^s R_t^s + A_t^b R_t^b + \widehat{w}_t - C_t - A_{t+1}^s - A_{t+1}^b \right] \\
&+ \lambda_{t+1} \left[A_{t+1}^s R_{t+1}^s + A_{t+1}^b R_{t+1}^b + \widehat{w}_{t+1} \right. \\
&\qquad\qquad \left. - C_{t+1} - A_{t+2}^s - A_{t+2}^b \right]. \qquad (3.26)
\end{aligned}
$$

To find the allocation that maximizes household utility, take derivatives with respect to each of the choice variables and set each derivative to zero:

$$
\begin{aligned}
C_t &: \quad 1/C_t &&= \quad \lambda_t \\
C_{t+1} &: \beta/C_{t+1} &&= \quad \lambda_{t+1} \\
A^s_{t+1} &: \quad \lambda_t &&= \quad \lambda_{t+1} R^s_{t+1} \\
A^b_{t+1} &: \quad \lambda_t &&= \quad \lambda_{t+1} R^b_{t+1}.
\end{aligned}
$$

When these four equations are combined, we uncover the relationship:

$$
0 = \beta \left[(C_t/C_{t+1}) * \left(R^s_{t+1} - R^b_{t+1} \right) \right]. \tag{3.27}
$$

If we divide both sides of equation (3.27) by β, and then allow for uncertainty in returns by appropriately including an expectations operator on the right-hand side, we produce equation (3.23):

$$
0 = E_t \left[(C_t/C_{t+1}) * \left(R^s_{t+1} - R^b_{t+1} \right) \right]. \tag{3.28}
$$

Discussion of Risk

Equation (3.28) does not imply that the expected return to stocks has to equal the expected return to Treasuries. Rather, it implies that the expected risk-adjusted return to stocks must equal the expected risk-adjusted return to Treasury Bills. We can rewrite equation (3.28) as

$$
E_t \left[(C_t/C_{t+1}) R^s_{t+1} \right] = E_t \left[(C_t/C_{t+1}) R^b_{t+1} \right]. \tag{3.29}
$$

The risk-adjustment factor on returns from our model is determined by the term (C_t/C_{t+1}), specifically the covariance of (C_t/C_{t+1}) with asset returns R^s_{t+1} and R^b_{t+1}. In other words, according to this model, the risk of an asset is related to how its payoff varies with (the inverse of) consumption growth.

For those of you that have had a course in statistics, recall that the expected value of the product of any two random variables X and Y is as follows:

$$E\,[XY] = E\,[X]\,E\,[Y] + \text{Cov}\,(X,\,Y), \qquad (3.30)$$

where Cov stands for the covariance of the two random variables X and Y. Suppose X and Y are two random variables, each with $t = 1, \ldots, T$ observations. Denote the sample average of X as $\bar{X}$ and the sample average of Y as $\bar{Y}$. Then, the estimate of the covariance of X and Y is

$$\text{Cov}\,(X,\,Y) = \frac{\sum\limits_{t=1}^{T} \left(X_t - \bar{X}\right)\left(Y_t - \bar{Y}\right)}{T - 1}.$$

In words, the covariance of two random variables describes how the variables tend to move together. For example, if the covariance of X and Y is greater than zero, then when X is above its average value, Y tends to be above its average value as well. If the covariance of X and Y is less than zero, then when X is above its average value, Y tends to be below its average value.[4]

The implications of equation (3.30) for equation (3.29) are as follows:

$$E_t\left[(C_t/C_{t+1})\,R_{t+1}^s\right] = E_t\left[C_t/C_{t+1}\right]E_t\left[R_{t+1}^s\right]$$
$$+ \text{Cov}\left(C_t/C_{t+1},\,R_{t+1}^s\right)$$

$$E_t\left[(C_t/C_{t+1})\,R_{t+1}^b\right] = E_t\left[C_t/C_{t+1}\right]E_t\left[R_{t+1}^b\right]$$
$$+ \text{Cov}\left(C_t/C_{t+1},\,R_{t+1}^b\right).$$

---

[4] We review this material again in Chapter 5.

Since $E_t\left[(C_t/C_{t+1})\,R^s_{t+1}\right] = E_t\left[(C_t/C_{t+1})\,R^b_{t+1}\right]$ from equation (3.29), after some algebra these equations imply:

$$E_t\left[R^s_{t+1}\right] = E_t\left[R^b_{t+1}\right]$$
$$+ \frac{\operatorname{Cov}\left(C_t/C_{t+1},\,R^b_{t+1}\right) - \operatorname{Cov}\left(C_t/C_{t+1},\,R^s_{t+1}\right)}{E_t\left[C_t/C_{t+1}\right]}.$$

This means that when there is uncertainty about returns, the expected return to stocks $E_t\left[R^s_{t+1}\right]$ is equal to the expected return to Treasuries $E_t\left[R^b_{t+1}\right]$ only when the risk of the two assets is identical. And the risk of the two assets is identical only when the covariance of the inverse of consumption growth with Treasury yields is equal to the covariance of the inverse of consumption growth with stock returns. When these covariances differ, stocks will pay a different expected return than Treasuries.

The Equity Premium Puzzle

Economists have tested equation (3.28) by defining a variable ϵ_{t+1} as

$$\epsilon_{t+1} = (C_t/C_{t+1}) * \left(R^s_{t+1} - R^b_{t+1}\right) \tag{3.31}$$

and evaluating whether ϵ_{t+1} has an average value of zero.[5] Figure 3.1 graphs ϵ_{t+1} over the 1949–2007 period. For C_t, I use per-capita real consumption exclusive of the real consumption of durable goods and for the excess return of stocks over Treasury Bills, $R^s_{t+1} - R^b_{t+1}$, I use

---

[5] For a recent paper employing a test like that of equation (3.31), see M. A. Davis, and R. F. Martin, 2009, "Housing, Home Production, and the Equity and Value Premium Puzzles," *Journal of Housing Economics*, forthcoming. The classic citation for the equity premium puzzle is R. Mehra and E. Prescott, 1985, "The Equity Premium: A Puzzle," *Journal of Monetary Economics*, vol. 15, pp. 145–161.

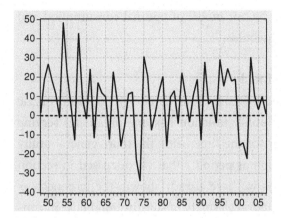

Figure 3.1 Realized values of ϵ_{t+1}, 1949–2007

data from Professor Kenneth French's website.[6] Note that I do not adjust the published excess returns for taxes.

The average value of ϵ_{t+1} over the 1949–2007 sample is 7.94 percent, shown by the solid straight line.[7] If equation (3.28) held, we would expect the average value of ϵ_{t+1} to be 0.0, shown by the dotted straight line.[8] The fact that the solid straight line is not close to zero means that we have an equity premium puzzle; that is, stock returns have been too high relative to the yield on Treasury Bills given the risk-adjustment

[6] The real consumption data are derived from the NIPA and the population data are taken from the BLS. The data on excess returns are available at http://mba.tuck. dartmouth.edu/pages/faculty/ken.french/data_library.html#HistBenchmarks. Click on one of the links (monthly/quarterly/annual) associated with the "Fama/French Benchmark Factors." The column heading "Rm-Rf" reports excess returns. These returns are computed as the value-weighted return on all NYSE, AMEX, and NASDAQ stocks less the one-month rate on Treasury Bills.

[7] For reference, the simple average of annual pre-tax excess returns over the 1949–2007 period is 8.12 percent.

[8] We cannot rule out the case that (3.28) held in expectation and before any shocks were realized, but after the full sequence of shocks was realized the average value of ϵ_{t+1} was positive. This is certainly possible, but improbable.

factor C_t/C_{t+1} implied by our model of optimal consumption and savings decisions of households.

Another Discussion of Risk

It is now acknowledged by some that the equity premium puzzle may arise because our utility function has one parameter serving two purposes. Consider for the time being the more general utility function for consumption at period t that we discussed in section 3.2.4, $C_t^{1-\sigma}/(1-\sigma)$. As we have already shown, the parameter σ determines the intertemporal elasticity of substitution between consumption at date t and consumption at date $t+1$ $(=-1/\sigma)$. σ, however, also determines households' aversion to risk of fluctuations in consumption in any given period; that is, it determines how much households are willing to pay to avoid uncertainty in the level of consumption in any period.

To see this, suppose that a household expects consumption to be $1.05 in period $t+1$ with a 50 percent probability and $0.95 with a 50 percent probability. Expected utility (i.e. the average level of utility, as discussed in section 3.2.6) from consumption in period $t+1$ is as follows

$$0.50 * \frac{1.05^{1-\sigma}}{1-\sigma} + 0.50 * \frac{0.95^{1-\sigma}}{1-\sigma}. \tag{3.32}$$

The first two columns of Table 3.1 list the level of expected utility computed using equation (3.32) for σ equal to three values: 1.5, 3.0, and 5.0. These are values of σ that are commonly used by macroeconomists and labor economists.[9] As Table 3.1 shows, expected utility of period $t+1$ consumption is negative because $1-\sigma$ is less than zero. This is not problematic: the level of utility can be negative – all that is required of our utility function is that the level of utility

---

[9] See Mehra and Prescott, "The Equity Premium."

Table 3.1 **Relationship of σ and risk aversion**		
σ	Expected utility	$\bar{C}_{t+1}$
1.5	−2.000	0.998
3.0	−0.504	0.996
5.0	−0.256	0.994

increases (i.e. becomes less negative) when the level of consumption increases.

The third column of this table, $\bar{C}_{t+1}$, shows the level of consumption in period $t + 1$ that provides the same (expected) utility if this level of consumption were to be provided with certainty. That is, in each row of the table, $\bar{C}_{t+1}$ solves

$$\frac{\bar{C}_{t+1}^{1-\sigma}}{1-\sigma} = 0.50 * \frac{1.05^{1-\sigma}}{1-\sigma} + 0.50 * \frac{0.95^{1-\sigma}}{1-\sigma}. \tag{3.33}$$

Notice that with the utility function we have written down, for the values of σ we consider, households are willing to forego a little risky consumption for a certain level of consumption. That is, consumption at $t + 1$, on average, is $1.0 = 0.5 * 1.05 + 0.5 * 0.95$. But, because the level of consumption in any period is uncertain – it is either 1.05 or 0.95 – households are willing to forego some consumption on average for certainty. This is known as "risk aversion." As the table shows, as σ increases, households are willing to forego more of their average level of consumption for certainty. In the case of $\sigma = 1.5$, households are willing to forego \$0.002 ($0.002 = 1.000 − 0.998$) of their average level of consumption; in the case of $\sigma = 5.0$, households are willing to forego \$0.006.

Thus, σ controls both households' willingness to substitute consumption across periods of time (the intertemporal elasticity of substitution) and households' aversion to uncertainty at any given period.

The fact that σ plays these two roles has been highlighted as a possible cause of the equity premium puzzle. A number of recent papers have added a parameter to the utility function that allows household risk aversion to be decoupled from the intertemporal elasticity of substitution. Although more work needs to be done, recent results are promising.[10]

3.3.2 Housing

In this section, we will assume that our household can save in period $t+1$ in one of two types of assets, financial assets A_{t+1} and rental housing H_{t+1}. Specifically, the budget constraint of the household at period t is

$$0 = A_t (1 + \widehat{r}_t) + \widehat{w}_t - C_t - A_{t+1} - p_t H_{t+1}. \tag{3.34}$$

To explain: in period t the household earns labor income $\widehat{w}_t$ and enters the period with some financial assets A_t that pay after-tax rate of return $\widehat{r}_t$. The household chooses period t consumption, period $t+1$ financial assets A_{t+1}, and the quantity of rental housing to carry to period $t+1$, H_{t+1}. The price per unit of rental housing is p_t.[11]

The budget constraint at period $t+1$ is

$$0 = A_{t+1} (1 + \widehat{r}_{t+1}) + (d_{t+1} + p_{t+1}) H_{t+1} + \widehat{w}_{t+1}$$
$$- C_{t+1} - A_{t+2} - p_{t+1} H_{t+2}. \tag{3.35}$$

Similar to period t, in period $t+1$ the household enters the period with some financial assets, A_{t+1}, that pay after-tax rate of return $\widehat{r}_{t+1}$.

---

[10] For a recent paper, see R. Bansal and A. Yaron, 2004, "Risks for the Long Run: A Potential Resolution of Asset Pricing Puzzles," *Journal of Finance*, vol. 59, pp. 1481–1509.

[11] Notice that the price of consumption is assumed to be 1.0. Thus, p_t is the price of one unit of rental housing relative to the price of one unit of consumption.

In addition, the household also owns H_{t+1} units of rental housing. If one unit of rental housing spins off d_{t+1} dollars of rent (net of taxes and expenses), then rental housing pays total after-tax rents of $d_{t+1} H_{t+1}$. The rental housing is valued at $p_{t+1} H_{t+1}$ after the rental income is paid out. The household chooses period $t + 1$ consumption, financial assets to carry forward to $t + 2$, and the value of rental housing to own in period $t + 2$.[12]

Households choose C_t, C_{t+1}, A_{t+1}, and H_{t+1} to maximize $\ln(C_t) + \beta \ln(C_{t+1})$ subject to the period t and period $t + 1$ budget constraints, equations (3.34) and (3.35). Denote the Lagrange multiplier on the period t budget constraint as λ_t and the Lagrange multiplier on the period $t + 1$ budget constraint as λ_{t+1}. To find the allocation that maximizes household utility, we take derivatives of

$$\ln(C_t) + \beta \ln(C_{t+1})$$
$$+ \lambda_t \left[A_t (1 + \widehat{r_t}) + \widehat{w}_t - C_t - A_{t+1} - p_t H_{t+1} \right]$$
$$+ \lambda_{t+1} \left[A_{t+1} (1 + \widehat{r}_{t+1}) + (d_{t+1} + p_{t+1}) H_{t+1} \right.$$
$$\left. + \widehat{w}_{t+1} - C_{t+1} - A_{t+2} - p_{t+1} H_{t+2} \right] \qquad (3.36)$$

with respect to each of the choices and set each derivative to zero. This process yields the following four first-order conditions:

$$
\begin{aligned}
C_t &: \quad 1/C_t &=& \quad \lambda_t \\
C_{t+1} &: \quad \beta/C_{t+1} &=& \quad \lambda_{t+1} \\
A_{t+1} &: \quad \lambda_t &=& \quad \lambda_{t+1}(1 + \widehat{r}_{t+1}) \\
H_{t+1} &: \quad \lambda_t p_t &=& \quad \lambda_{t+1}(d_{t+1} + p_{t+1}).
\end{aligned}
$$

---

[12] As mentioned earlier, the analysis of this and earlier sections does not depend in any meaningful way on the assumption that a household lives for only two periods.

Now substitute for λ_t and λ_{t+1} using the first two equations and rewrite the last two equations as:

$$1 = \beta\,(C_t/C_{t+1})\,(1 + \widehat{r}_{t+1}) \tag{3.37}$$

$$1 = \beta\,(C_t/C_{t+1})\,(1 + d_{t+1}/p_t + g_{t+1})\,. \tag{3.38}$$

In equation (3.38), g_{t+1} stands for the real capital gain in housing, such that $p_{t+1}/p_t \equiv 1 + g_{t+1}$.[13]

Comparing equation (3.37) with equation (3.38) naturally leads us to define the return to housing $\widehat{r}^h_{t+1}$ as the sum of the "dividend yield" on rental housing d_{t+1}/p_t plus the real capital gain to housing:

$$\widehat{r}^h_{t+1} = d_{t+1}/p_t + g_{t+1}\,. \tag{3.39}$$

Notice the definition of the dividend yield: the purchase of one unit of housing, at cost of p_t, yields d_{t+1} worth of dividends, which are net rents in the case of housing. Or, in other words, the purchase of one dollar's worth of housing yields d_{t+1}/p_t dollars of dividends.

Subtracting equation (3.38) from (3.37) yields the following expression:

$$0 = (C_t/C_{t+1})\,(\widehat{r}_{t+1} - \widehat{r}^h_{t+1})\,.$$

When returns are uncertain, the above expression becomes

$$0 = E_t\left[(C_t/C_{t+1})\,(\widehat{r}_{t+1} - \widehat{r}^h_{t+1})\right]. \tag{3.40}$$

This is analogous to the result of the previous section for stocks and Treasuries: if households are to simultaneously invest in two assets, then the risk-adjusted expected return of the assets must be identical.

---

[13] Since the price of consumption is always 1.0, p_{t+1}/p_t is the real (inflation-adjusted) growth rate in the price of housing.

Rental vs. Owner-Occupied Housing

Although the analysis of the previous section was concerned with the decision to purchase (invest in) rental housing, the exact same analysis holds for the decision to buy and live in owner-occupied housing. The only thing that changes is the interpretation of the $d_{t+1} H_{t+1}$ term. In the case of rental housing, $d_{t+1} H_{t+1}$ stands for total rental income that is collected from tenants, net of maintenance and taxes. In the case of owner-occupied housing, $d_{t+1} H_{t+1}$ is the value to the owner of living in H_{t+1} units of owner-occupied housing for one period. It can be thought of as the amount the owner would be willing to pay to rent the house, less maintenance expenses and any property tax payments. Other than that, the analysis of rental and owner-occupied is identical. As a result, throughout this section we identify $\widehat{r}_{t+1}^h$ as simply the "return to housing."

The Price Level for Housing

Return to equations (3.38) and (3.39), and recall that $g_{t+1} = p_{t+1}/p_t - 1$, implying

$$1 + \widehat{r}_{t+1}^h = \frac{d_{t+1}}{p_t} + \frac{p_{t+1}}{p_t}.$$

Multiply this equation by p_t and divide by $1 + \widehat{r}_{t+1}^h$ to get

$$p_t = \frac{d_{t+1}}{\left(1 + \widehat{r}_{t+1}^h\right)} + \frac{p_{t+1}}{\left(1 + \widehat{r}_{t+1}^h\right)}. \tag{3.41}$$

Note that the above equation also holds at period $t + 1$ implying

$$p_{t+1} = \frac{d_{t+2}}{\left(1 + \widehat{r}_{t+2}^h\right)} + \frac{p_{t+2}}{\left(1 + \widehat{r}_{t+2}^h\right)}.$$

Now divide both sides by $1 + \widehat{r}_{t+1}^h$:

$$\frac{p_{t+1}}{\left(1 + \widehat{r}_{t+1}^h\right)} = \frac{d_{t+2}}{\left(1 + \widehat{r}_{t+1}^h\right)\left(1 + \widehat{r}_{t+2}^h\right)} + \frac{p_{t+2}}{\left(1 + \widehat{r}_{t+1}^h\right)\left(1 + \widehat{r}_{t+2}^h\right)}. \tag{3.42}$$

Finally, insert equation (3.42) into equation (3.41) to yield

$$p_t = \frac{d_{t+1}}{\left(1 + \hat{r}_{t+1}^h\right)} + \frac{d_{t+2}}{\left(1 + \hat{r}_{t+1}^h\right)\left(1 + \hat{r}_{t+2}^h\right)}$$
$$+ \frac{p_{t+2}}{\left(1 + \hat{r}_{t+1}^h\right)\left(1 + \hat{r}_{t+2}^h\right)}. \quad (3.43)$$

Suppose for simplicity that the required return to housing is fixed over time at $\hat{r}^h$, such that

$$\hat{r}_{t+1}^h = \hat{r}_{t+2}^h = \ldots = \hat{r}_{t+i}^h = \hat{r}^h$$

for any i. Then (3.43) can be rewritten as

$$p_t = \frac{d_{t+1}}{\left(1 + \hat{r}^h\right)} + \frac{d_{t+2}}{\left(1 + \hat{r}^h\right)^2} + \frac{p_{t+2}}{\left(1 + \hat{r}^h\right)^2}. \quad (3.44)$$

We can continue substituting for p_{t+2}, p_{t+3}, etc. into equation (3.44) using the same technique we employed in equation (3.42). After substitution, this yields the expression

$$p_t = \frac{d_{t+1}}{\left(1 + \hat{r}^h\right)} + \frac{d_{t+2}}{\left(1 + \hat{r}^h\right)^2} + \frac{d_{t+3}}{\left(1 + \hat{r}^h\right)^3} + \frac{d_{t+4}}{\left(1 + \hat{r}^h\right)^4} + \ldots$$

$$(3.45)$$

In words, equation (3.45) states that the price of a house is equal to the appropriately discounted infinite sum of its rents, and the discount rate is the required return to housing.

The Growth Rate of House Prices and Housing Rents

Suppose now that rents increase at a constant rate, call it γ, such that

$$d_{t+1} = d_t (1 + \gamma)$$

$$d_{t+2} = d_{t+1} (1 + \gamma)$$

$$d_{t+3} = d_{t+2} (1 + \gamma)$$

and so forth. After substitutions, equation (3.45) can be rewritten as

$$p_t = \frac{d_{t+1}}{1+\widehat{r}^h}\left[1 + \frac{(1+\gamma)}{(1+\widehat{r}^h)} + \frac{(1+\gamma)^2}{(1+\widehat{r}^h)^2} + \frac{(1+\gamma)^3}{(1+\widehat{r}^h)^3} + \dots\right].$$

$$(3.46)$$

We can rewrite the above term in brackets using mathematical notation for an infinite sum as[14]

$$p_t = \frac{d_{t+1}}{1+\widehat{r}^h}\sum_{s=0}^{\infty}\left(\frac{1+\gamma}{1+\widehat{r}^h}\right)^s.$$

$$(3.47)$$

As long as $\gamma < \widehat{r}^h$, then it can be shown that

$$\sum_{s=0}^{\infty}\left(\frac{1+\gamma}{1+\widehat{r}^h}\right)^s = \frac{1}{1-\frac{1+\gamma}{1+\widehat{r}^h}} = \frac{1+\widehat{r}^h}{\widehat{r}^h-\gamma}.$$

$$(3.48)$$

Inserting equation (3.48) into (3.47) yields

$$p_t = \left(\frac{d_{t+1}}{1+\widehat{r}^h}\right)\left(\frac{1+\widehat{r}^h}{\widehat{r}^h-\gamma}\right) = \frac{d_{t+1}}{\widehat{r}^h-\gamma}.$$

This implies

$$\frac{p_t}{d_{t+1}} = \frac{1}{\widehat{r}^h-\gamma}$$

and thus

$$d_{t+1}/p_t = \widehat{r}^h - \gamma$$
$$\text{and } \widehat{r}^h = d_{t+1}/p_t + \gamma.$$

$$(3.49)$$

For convenience, we rewrite equations (3.39) and (3.49) below:

$$\widehat{r}_{t+1}^h = d_{t+1}/p_t + g_{t+1}$$

$$(3.50)$$

$$\widehat{r}^h = d_{t+1}/p_t + \gamma.$$

$$(3.51)$$

---

[14] Recall that any number raised to the 0 power is equal to 1.0.

Equation (3.50) defines realized housing returns in period $t + 1$ ($\widehat{r}_{t+1}^h$) as the sum of the dividend yield (d_{t+1}/p_t) and the capital gain on house prices (g_{t+1}); equation (3.51) shows the relationship between required returns to housing ($\widehat{r}^h$), the growth rate of dividends (γ), and the dividend yield when the required return to housing and the growth rate of dividends are fixed over time. This analysis suggests that the growth rate of house prices g_{t+1}, on average, should reflect the growth rate of housing rents, γ.

The Rent-Price Ratio for Housing

Returning to equation (3.50), rearrange terms and express the dividend yield for housing as the total return to housing less the capital gain to housing, i.e.

$$\frac{d_{t+1}}{p_t} = \widehat{r}_{t+1}^h - g_{t+1}. \tag{3.52}$$

Because the dividend for housing is rents net of expenses and taxes, the dividend yield for housing is commonly called the "rent-price ratio" or sometimes the "ratio of rents to prices."[15]

Suppose that two housing units have different ratios of rents to prices. We can then infer that either (a) the required return to the two housing units, $\widehat{r}_{t+1}^h$, differs or (b) the expected rate of future capital gains g_{t+1} differs between the two units. Units with relatively low required returns or high expected growth in prices will have relatively low rent-price ratios.

These ideas help to explain why house prices in certain metropolitan areas seem very high relative to the cost of renting in the same

---

[15] Real-estate professionals also refer to this ratio as the "cap rate." For more information consult R. K. Green and S. Malpezzi, 2003, *A Primer on US Housing Markets and Housing Policy*, Washington, DC: Urban Institute Press. The American Real Estate and Urban Economics Association.

Table 3.2 **Rent-price ratio by MSA, 2000**			
Midwest	Rent-price ratio	Northeast	Rent-price ratio
Chicago	4.4%	Boston	3.4%
Cincinnati	4.4%	New York	3.4%
Cleveland	4.9%	Philadelphia	5.2%
Detroit	4.1%	Pittsburgh	5.2%
Kansas City	5.5%		
Milwaukee	4.5%		
Minneapolis	5.3%		
St. Louis	5.1%		
South	Rent-price ratio	West	Rent-price ratio
Atlanta	5.2%	Denver	5.5%
Dallas	6.2%	Honolulu	3.3%
Houston	6.6%	Los Angeles	3.6%
Miami	5.1%	Portland	4.7%
		San Diego	4.0%
		San Francisco	3.2%
		Seattle	4.5%

metropolitan area. In a recent paper, my co-authors and I use data from the 2000 Decennial Census of Housing to estimate the ratio of annual rents to house prices in the year 2000 for 23 metropolitan areas across the US.[16] In Table 3.2 I report the estimates for the 23 US metropolitan areas (MSAs), sorted by census region. These estimates do not net out tax payments or expenditures for maintenance.[17]

Table 3.2 shows that in mid-year 2000 the rent-price ratio ranged from 3.2 percent in San Francisco to 6.6 percent in Houston, with an average of 4.7 percent across metropolitan areas. Suppose that the required return to housing is constant across metro areas. Then,

[16] See S. Campbell, M. Davis, J. Gallin, and R. Martin, 2008, "What Moves Housing Markets: A Variance Decomposition of the Rent-Price Ratio," Working Paper, University of Wisconsin-Madison.

[17] These data are available at http://morris.marginalq.com/whatmoves.html.

Table 3.3 Comparison of rent-price ratio by MSA in 2000 with growth in house prices from 2000 to 2007

Metro area	Rent-price ratio 2000:2	Growth in house prices 2000:2–2007:4
San Francisco	3.2%	69.1%
Honolulu	3.3%	128.4%
New York	3.4%	100.7%
Kansas City	5.5%	34.0%
Dallas	6.2%	28.5%
Houston	6.6%	39.4%

based on our theory, areas with low rent-price ratios should have experienced the fastest growth in house prices.

Table 3.3 reports the three lowest and three highest values of the rent-price ratio in 2000, and subsequent growth in house prices from mid-year 2000 through year-end 2007. Although the correlation is not perfect, this table illustrates that areas with relatively low rent-price ratios as of mid-year 2000 experienced relatively fast growth in house prices in 2000–2007. Unless the required returns to housing $(\widehat{r}^h_{t+1})$ vary across metropolitan areas, the price level of housing must be high (relative to rental value) in metropolitan areas in which residents expect relatively robust capital gains. Otherwise, residents in these areas would receive higher-than-required returns to housing.

The same ideas can be used to help analyze changes to the rent-price ratio over time for a fixed geographic area. If we notice that the rent-price ratio (d_{t+1}/p_{t+1}) of a given geographic area does not change, then we may infer that the required return to housing less the expected capital gain to housing, $\widehat{r}_{t+1} - g_{t+1}$, has not changed. If the

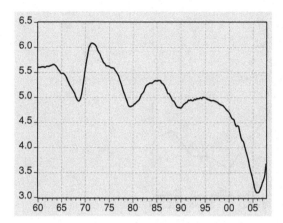

Figure 3.2 Ratio of annual rents to house prices (percent), 1960:1–2007:4

rent-price ratio changes for a given area, however, then we can infer that either $\widehat{r}_{t+1}$ or g_{t+1} has changed.[18]

Figure 3.2 plots an estimate of the rent-price ratio for the aggregate US using data that my co-authors and I have recently developed.[19] This figure clearly shows that during the housing boom in the US that occurred between 1997 and 2006, the ratio of rents to house prices in the United States fell quite dramatically. From this data, we can infer that over this period either the required return to housing fell, or the expected future capital gain to house prices increased, or both.

[18] This statement is only approximately true. The exact statement is that the expected net present value of $\widehat{r}_{t+1}$ less the expected net present value of g_{t+1} has changed. See J. Y. Campbell and R. J. Shiller, 1988, "The Dividend-Price Ratio and Expectations of Future Dividends and Discount Factors," *Review of Financial Studies*, vol. 1, pp. 195–228.

[19] Like the data in Table 3.2, these estimates do not net out tax payments or expenditures on maintenance. See M. A. Davis, A. Lehnert, and R. F. Martin, 2008, "The Rent-Price Ratio for the Aggregate Stock of Owner-Occupied Housing," *Review of Income and Wealth*, vol. 54, pp. 279–284. The source data for this graph are available on my website at http://morris.marginalq.com/dlm_data. html.

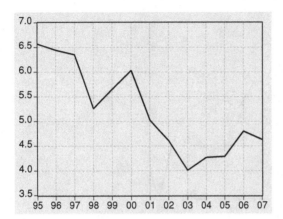

Figure 3.3 Nominal interest rate on 10-year Treasury Bonds, 1995–2007

Although we do not have direct data on expected future capital gains, we have some evidence that the required return to housing may have fallen over this period. Recall that our models imply that risk-adjusted expected returns to all assets must be identical. Shown in Figure 3.3, over the 1995–2007 period, the nominal interest rate on 10-year Treasury Bonds fell by about 1.5 percentage points, from about 6 percent over the 1995–2000 period to 4.5 percent over the 2003–2007 period.[20] Suppose that inflation expectations did not change over this period, such that the 1.5 percentage point decline in 10-year Treasury Bonds that occurred over this period represents a real decline.[21] If the real return to housing $\widehat{r}_t^h = d_{t+1}/p_t + g_{t+1}$ also fell by 1.5 percentage points – in line with the 10-year Treasury – and the entire decline in housing returns was manifest in a decline in the rent-price ratio (d_{t+1}/p_t) and not in a decline in the expected

[20] The data graphed in figure 3.3 are taken from www.federalreserve.gov/releases/ h15/data/Annual/H15_TCMNOM_Y10.txt.

[21] For example, if inflation expectations had declined by 0.5 percentage points over this period, then the real 10-year Treasury yield would have fallen by 1.0 percentage points = 1.5 percent nominal decline less 0.5 percent decline in expected inflation.

growth rate of capital gains (g_{t+1}), then much or maybe all of the rise in house prices during the 1997–2006 housing boom can be justified. The logic is as follows: the real return on a 10-year Treasury fell; housing must pay the same risk-adjusted return as the 10-year Treasury; and, assuming the expected capital gains to housing did not change, house prices increased faster than rents, driving down the rent-price ratio and reducing the return to housing.

That said, the analysis of the previous paragraph should not be interpreted as suggesting that the full change in house prices over the 1997–2006 period is explainable using standard asset-pricing techniques. Among those "in the know," the debate about whether or not there was a house price "bubble" in the 1997–2006 housing boom is actually about whether house prices increased to the "right" level given the observed decline in returns on 10-year Treasury Bonds. To explain: it is not clear that any change in housing returns should have occurred exclusively in d_{t+1}/p_t; that is, why shouldn't g_{t+1} also have changed? Second, prior to 1996, the available data indicate that the required return to housing was largely uncorrelated with the return on 10-year Treasury Bonds. It is not clear why that relationship would have changed after 1997.[22]

3.4 Optimal Labor, Consumption, Investment

3.4.1 Model

In this last section of the chapter, we study the optimal labor supply decision of households when they also choose consumption and investment. That is, we merge the first part of the chapter, the

---

[22] See Campbell *et al.* "What Moves Housing Markets."

labor-supply decision when households have no savings, with the second part of the chapter, the savings decision when household labor supply is fixed.

As before, we assume households live two periods, t and $t+1$, and enter period t with a stock of assets denoted A_t. Households choose consumption and the quantity of labor to supply to the market in both periods. The after-tax wage rate per unit of labor supplied in t and $t+1$ is $\widehat{w}_t$ and $\widehat{w}_{t+1}$, respectively.

Households are assumed to receive the following lifetime utility from consumption and leisure in t and $t+1$:

$$\theta \ln(C_t) + (1-\theta)\ln(1-L_t)$$
$$+ \beta\left[\theta \ln(C_{t+1}) + (1-\theta)\ln(1-L_{t+1})\right]. \quad (3.53)$$

One interpretation of the above is that lifetime utility is equal to the sum of utility from consumption and leisure in t, $\theta \ln(C_t) + (1-\theta)\ln(1-L_t)$, and discounted utility from consumption and leisure in $t+1$, $\beta\left[\theta \ln(C_{t+1}) + (1-\theta)\ln(1-L_{t+1})\right]$. In period t, the household chooses C_t, C_{t+1}, L_t, and L_{t+1} to maximize lifetime utility. Notice that leisure in t is defined as $1-L_t$ and leisure in $t+1$ is defined as $1-L_{t+1}$. L_t therefore represents the fraction of the day (excluding time spent sleeping) that people spend working and $1-L_t$ stands for the fraction of the day that people spend in leisure activities. This is consistent with a total time endowment of one day in which people either take leisure or work.

The budget constraints at time t and $t+1$ are

$$A_t(1+\widehat{r}_t) + \widehat{w}_t L_t - C_t - A_{t+1} = 0$$
$$A_{t+1}(1+\widehat{r}_{t+1}) + \widehat{w}_{t+1} L_{t+1} - C_{t+1} - A_{t+2} = 0.$$

Combining these budget constraints yields a unified budget constraint of:

$$A_t(1 + \widehat{r}_t) + \widehat{w}_t L_t - C_t - \frac{1}{1 + \widehat{r}_{t+1}}$$
$$(A_{t+2} + C_{t+1} - \widehat{w}_{t+1} L_{t+1}) = 0.$$

To find the optimal choices of C_t, C_{t+1}, L_t, and L_{t+1}, we use the Lagrange multiplier technique. That is, we set the derivatives of

$$\theta \ln(C_t) + (1 - \theta)\ln(1 - L_t) + \beta[\theta \ln(C_{t+1})$$
$$+ (1 - \theta)\ln(1 - L_{t+1})]$$
$$+ \lambda\left[A_t(1 + \widehat{r}_t) + \widehat{w}_t L_t - C_t - \frac{1}{1 + \widehat{r}_{t+1}}(A_{t+2}\right.$$
$$\left. + C_{t+1} - \widehat{w}_{t+1} L_{t+1})\right]$$

with respect to the choices C_t, C_{t+1}, L_t, and L_{t+1} equal to zero.

Taking the derivatives with respect to C_t and C_{t+1} and setting these derivatives to zero yields

$$\theta/C_t = \lambda$$
$$\beta * \theta/C_{t+1} = \lambda/(1 + \widehat{r}_{t+1}).$$

When these two equations are combined and redundant variables are eliminated, we uncover the familiar solution

$$\frac{C_{t+1}}{C_t} = \beta(1 + \widehat{r}_{t+1}),$$

which is exactly the solution we achieved in the model of optimal savings that had no labor supply decision. This does not mean that labor supply does not affect the level of consumption. It just means that it does not affect the relationship between consumption at t and consumption at $t + 1$ – in this model that relationship is entirely determined by the preference parameter β and by the after-tax rate of return on assets $\widehat{r}_{t+1}$.

The derivatives with respect to labor supply at period t and $t+1$, L_t and L_{t+1} are:

$$(1 - \theta)/(1 - L_t) = \lambda \widehat{w}_t$$

$$\beta (1 - \theta)/(1 - L_{t+1}) = \lambda \widehat{w}_{t+1}/(1 + \widehat{r}_{t+1}).$$

These two equations can be combined as

$$\frac{1 - L_{t+1}}{1 - L_t} = \beta (1 + \widehat{r}_{t+1}) * \frac{\widehat{w}_t}{\widehat{w}_{t+1}}. \tag{3.54}$$

Equation (3.54) shows that optimal labor supply decisions can vary and depend on wages! This result contrasts with the results of the labor supply model we wrote down at the start of this chapter, where labor supply was fixed regardless of the wage. In sum, by adding an investment decision to the static labor supply model of earlier in the chapter, we have linked changes in labor supply to changes in wages.

To understand how equation (3.54) implies that household labor supply varies with wages, suppose that

$$\beta (1 + \widehat{r}_{t+1}) * \frac{\widehat{w}_t}{\widehat{w}_{t+1}} > 1,$$

which implies that after-tax wage rates in period $t+1$ are expected to fall relative to after-tax wage rates in period t, once the period t wage is weighted by $\beta (1 + \widehat{r}_{t+1})$. This implies, via equation (3.54), that

$$\frac{1 - L_{t+1}}{1 - L_t} > 1.$$

This can only be true when $L_t > L_{t+1}$. Therefore, this model predicts a positive correlation of labor supply and wages, holding interest rates fixed: labor supply in period t is larger than labor supply in period $t + 1$ if hourly wages in period t are sufficiently greater than hourly wages in period $t + 1$.

3.4.2 Calibration

To conclude this chapter, we use equation (3.54) to "calibrate" the utility function parameter β. Loosely speaking, we calibrate a model by choosing parameters such as β to align the predictions of the model with data on hand.

The following gives an example of how macroeconomists calibrate models in practice: we know that, on average in the postwar period, hours worked per capita in the US are trendless, which suggests that the average value of the left-hand side of (3.54), $(1 - L_{t+1}) / (1 - L_t)$, is 1.0. This means the average value of the right-hand side of (3.54) is 1.0 as well:

$$\beta (1 + \widehat{r}_{t+1}) * \frac{\widehat{w}_t}{\widehat{w}_{t+1}} = 1.0,$$

which implies

$$\beta = \left(\frac{1.0}{1 + \widehat{r}_{t+1}} \right) \left(\frac{\widehat{w}_{t+1}}{\widehat{w}_t} \right).$$

Suppose available data suggest the average annual after-tax return on the economy-wide stock of assets is 6 percent, implying $(1 + \widehat{r}_{t+1}) = 1.06$. Given that labor income is a constant $(1 - \alpha)$ share of GDP (see Chapter 1) and per-capita hours worked are trendless, and assuming that the tax rate on labor income is trendless, we can set the average value of $\widehat{w}_{t+1}/\widehat{w}_t$ equal to 1 plus the growth rate of annual per-capita real GDP, 1.019.[23] Thus, a calibrated estimate of β appropriate for a model of annual decision-making that is consistent with our data and theory is:

$$\beta = \left(\frac{1.0}{1.06} \right) (1.019) = 0.96.$$

This is a standard value of β that is used in macroeconomic and asset-pricing models.

FURTHER READING

- "Assets," as measured by the BEA, and treated by many economists as the total productive stock of capital (K_t), is not conceptually the same as household "wealth" (A_t). The difference is that assets, as measured by the BEA, include only built assets, such as machines and structures. This means that any change in asset prices due to changes in the price of non-built capital – such as the value of patents and intellectual property in the case of corporations, and the value of land and location in the case of housing – is not counted by the BEA as a change in the amount of capital.

  Household wealth is estimated by the Federal Reserve Board and published in the *Flow of Funds Accounts of the United States*. The Flow of Funds data are available at www.federalreserve.gov/releases/z1/. The specific table within the Flow of Funds data that lists the components of household wealth is B.100. According to line 42 of this table, total net worth of households (A_t) as of year-end 2006 was $55.7 trillion. For comparison, the BEA estimates total private capital – K_t excluding government assets but inclusive

---

[23] That is, the growth rate of real per-capita GDP is 1.9 percent. Recall that $w_t L_t = (1 - \alpha) Y_t = (1 - \alpha) GDP_t$.

of the stock of residential structures and consumer durables – at year-end 2006 to have been $35.7 trillion.

My own research with Jonathan Heathcote suggests that $10.4 trillion of this $20 trillion dollar gap between A_t and K_t is attributable to the value of residential locations and land. For more details, see M. A. Davis and J. Heathcote, 2007, "The Price and Quantity of Residential Land in the United States," *Journal of Monetary Economics*, vol. 54, pp. 2595–2620.

- There is a relatively new strand of economics called "behavioral economics" that deviates a bit from the rational expectations and time-consistent paradigm that we used in this chapter. Behavioral economists attempt to mix ideas in medicine and psychology with results from experimental economics to better understand if (or how) human beings systematically deviate in decision-making from rational expectations or time-consistent behavior. This is not my cup of tea for a number of reasons, but interested readers can find out more about the field from Wikipedia, http://en.wikipedia.org/wiki/Behavioural_economics. More advanced readers may also want to consult an article by W. Pesendorfer, 2006, "Behavioral Economics Comes of Age: A Review Essay on Advances in Behavioral Economics," *Journal of Economic Literature*, vol. 44, pp. 712–721, available in working paper form at www.princeton.edu/~pesendor/book-review.pdf.

H Homework

1 Suppose in 2000 that the dividend yield on IBM is 5 percent (annual) and that dividends always increase by 3 percent per year.

a. At what rate are investors discounting future dividends?

b. Now suppose that between 2000 and 2001, the dividend increased by 3 percent (as expected) but the price of IBM increased by 5 percent. Also assume that expected future dividend growth has not changed. What is the new dividend yeild for IBM? At what rate are investors discounting future dividends?

2 You have been told the ratio of annual rents to house prices (the "dividend yield" for housing) is 5 percent in 2000. You also have access to a nominal rent index ("BLS"), a nominal house price index ("HPI"), and a consumer-price index ("CPI") for 2000–2002 as follows:

Year	BLS	HPI	CPI
2000	135.0	226.3	56.0
2001	140.4	237.6	57.4
2002	143.2	249.5	59.1

a. Compute the dividend yield for housing in 2001 and 2002. Make sure you show work.

b. Compute the real (adjusted for CPI growth) capital gain to housing for 2000–2001 and then for 2001–2002. Make sure you show work.

c. Compute the total real (adjusted for CPI growth) return to housing in 2000–2001 and then 2001–2002. Make sure you show work.

3 Suppose the rent-price ratio for housing in Madison, Wisconsin is 8 percent and there is a property tax of 2.5 percent of the value of housing. What is the effective tax rate on rental income accruing to owner-occupiers?

Now suppose that prices have surged relative to rents (due to a change in the discount factor that owner-occupiers apply to the flow of implicit rents), so the new rent-price ratio in Madison is 6 percent. Holding the property-tax rate fixed at 2.5 percent, what is the new effective tax rate on rental income accruing to owner-occupiers?

4 It has been noticed that in the past century in the US we have spent roughly 20 hours a week per person engaged in market-based work. Assume that we have roughly $7 * 15 = 105$ hours per week of discretionary (non-sleep and non-personal-care) time. Assume (i) people have no saving, (ii) preferences for consumption (C) and leisure (N) are of the form

$$\theta \ln(C) + (1 - \theta) \ln(N),$$

and (iii) people are subject to two constraints: a budget constraint of

$$w * L - C = 0$$

(where L is hours worked) and a weekly time constraint of

$$105 - L - N = 0.$$

What do the data suggest is the value of θ? Make sure you either derive or explain your answer.

5 François is assumed to have a utility function from consumption c and leisure n of

$$\theta \ln(c) + (1 - \theta) \ln(n).$$

François receives labor income equal to his daily after-tax wage rate $\hat{w}$ times the fraction of each day that he works l. Because François is French, he also receives transfer income from the government that he does not earn equal to τ. François receives this income regardless of the amount of time he spends working. François allocates his non-personal-care time each day to either enjoying leisure or working. In summary, François has the following budget and time constraints:

Budget constraint: $\tau + \hat{w}l - c = 0$
Time constraint: $1 - n - l = 0.$

Determine how François's optimal time spent working l varies with his after-tax wage rate $\hat{w}$ and the amount of transfer income τ from the government.

6 A household has income today of \$100. The income can be spent either on current consumption c_t or future consumption c_{t+1}. Income that is not spent on current consumption earns a rate of return of 10 percent.

   a. Write down the household's budget constraint.
   b. What is the price of consumption today relative to the price of future consumption?

7 Assume François lives for two periods, t and $t + 1$. François is assumed to have a utility function of

$$\ln(C_t) + \beta \ln(C_{t+1}).$$

François starts period t with assets of A_t that earn rate of return r_t during period t. Because he is French, François also receives income from the government during period t of Y_t (that he did not earn), but receives no income during period $t + 1$.

François's problem is to choose C_t, C_{t+1}, and A_{t+1} to maximize utility.

   a. Write down the intertemporal period t budget constraint that links A_t, r_t, Y_t, and C_t with A_{t+1}.
   b. Using the Lagrange multiplier technique, derive the expression linking optimal consumption at time t and at time $t + 1$ with the interest rate on assets at time t, r_t, and the preference parameter β.

8 A household lives for two periods, receives labor income of $\widehat{w}_t$ in period t and $\widehat{w}_{t+1}$ in period $t + 1$, and has no preference for leisure. Suppose that the remaining lifetime utility of household members has the form:

$$\frac{C_t^{1-\sigma}}{1-\sigma} + \beta \frac{C_{t+1}^{1-\sigma}}{1-\sigma}.$$

Show that the optimal solution for consumption at periods t and $t + 1$ has the form

$$1 = \beta \left(\frac{C_t}{C_{t+1}} \right)^{\sigma} (1 + \widehat{r}_{t+1}).$$

9 Consider the pricing kernel for assets implied by the solution of the previous problem of

$$m_t = \beta \left(\frac{C_t}{C_{t+1}} \right)^{\sigma}.$$

Download data on aggregate annual real consumption and annual population and construct real per-capita consumption. Then download the historical data on the excess returns to stocks over

Treasuries. Once this is done, determine the value of σ required such that the average value of

$$\left(\frac{C_t}{C_{t+1}}\right)^{\sigma} \left(R_{t+1}^s - R_{t+1}^b\right)$$

is equal to 0 over the 1947:1–2007:4 period.

4 | Trade

O　Objectives of this Chapter

We start this chapter by introducing the idea of comparative advantage to describe why two people named Bjørn and François may want to trade. The example shows that when people have different skills in the production of two goods, both can enjoy an increase in their standard of living if they specialize in the production of the good in which they have a relative cost advantage (i.e. a comparative advantage) and then trade. This outcome is possible because, when people have different skills, specialization is efficient and leads to higher total output. The example highlights the potential benefits of any kind of specialization and trade: Bjørn and François can be two neighbors in the same community or can represent the working populations of two countries such as Norway and France.

The chapter continues by noting that trade does not always involve (on-net) exchange of goods for goods, but sometimes goods for assets. We introduce the idea of current accounts (surplus or deficit of goods-for-goods trade) and capital accounts (surplus or deficit of assets-for-assets trade) and describe why simple accounting requires that the current and capital accounts sum to zero. We then show data on the current account – exports, imports, and net exports – in the US in 1929–2007.

The next section of the chapter describes why people (and by extension countries) may find it beneficial to trade goods for assets. The intuition is straightforward and linked to the previous example in the chapter. Suppose there are two goods called "consumption today" and "future consumption," and further suppose that residents of one country are relatively more efficient than a second country at producing current consumption rather than future consumption.[1] In this scenario, residents of the two countries will find it advantageous to specialize in production and trade current consumption for financial assets or vice versa. Since financial assets are claims to future consumption, the trading of current consumption for financial assets is, in effect, a trade of current consumption for future consumption.

The chapter ends with a discussion of the impact of trade on factor prices and exchange rates. First, we determine the impact of free trade on the wage rate paid to labor when capital is mobile and labor is not. We show that wage rates rise (fall) if the domestic rate of return on capital is higher (lower) than the worldwide rate prior to trade. Then, we discuss three ideas related to exchange rates: covered interest parity, purchasing power parity, and the Fisher equation. Covered interest parity describes a relationship between spot and future exchange rates that ensures that traders cannot make profits by exploiting differences in nominal interest rates across countries. Purchasing power parity suggests that (under certain conditions) the current exchange rate between two countries must be reflective of the relative price level of tradable goods in those countries, otherwise traders cannot make profits by buying goods in one country and reselling them in another country. Finally, the Fisher equation describes the relationship between nominal interest rates, real interest rates, and inflation. We use an example to show that the Fisher equation is consistent with both the covered interest parity and purchasing power parity conditions.

---

[1] That is, the residents have a comparative advantage in producing current consumption. We show that this comparative advantage exists whenever the rate of return on savings is different in the two countries.

4.1 Trade of Goods for Goods

Table 4.1 **Bjørn and François** **production possibilities**		
	Bjørn	François
Guitar riffs	10/hour	7/hour
French food	8/hour	6/hour

Economics is the study of allocations; allocations arise from exchange between agents, and exchange is trade. In many ways, trade *is* economics.

Consider the following example of two regular guys named Bjørn and François. Bjørn and François like to consume sweet guitar riffs and delicious plates of French food and both are capable of producing these two items with some degree of competence. Bjørn and François are not identical in their skills, and they are able to produce guitar riffs and French food according to the production schedule shown in Table 4.1.

One feasible allocation would involve Bjørn and François living in "autarky." Autarky is a situation in which no exchange occurs: Bjørn and François would each produce some guitar riffs and some French food and both would consume exactly what they produce. Suppose in autarky that Bjørn and François each spend half of the eight-hour work day making guitar riffs and half making food. Bjørn would produce and consume 40 guitar riffs and 32 plates of French food and François would produce and consume 28 guitar riffs and 24 plates of French food – see Table 4.2. The total output of the efforts of Bjørn and François in autarky is 68 guitar riffs and 56 plates of French food.

Now, can Bjørn and François both improve their standard of living? The answer is "yes" as long as Bjørn and François specialize somewhat

Table 4.2 **Bjørn and François production: autarky**

	Bjørn			François			
	Output per hour	Hours	Total	Output per hour	Hours	Total	Total
Guitar riffs	10	4	40	7	4	28	68
French food	8	4	32	6	4	24	56

Table 4.3 **Bjørn and François production with some specialization**

	Bjørn			François			
	Output per hour	Hours	Total	Output per hour	Hours	Total	Total
Guitar riffs	10	5	50	7	$2\frac{2}{3}$	$18\frac{2}{3}$	$68\frac{2}{3}$
French food	8	3	24	6	$5\frac{1}{3}$	32	56

in production and both are willing to exchange guitar riffs for food (and vice versa). You might think that Bjørn would not find it worthwhile to exchange anything with François since Bjørn can produce more guitar riffs and more plates of food than François in any given hour. However, both Bjørn and François can enjoy a better lifestyle if they specialize in production and agree to exchange goods.

Consider a scenario where (a) Bjørn spends one less hour cooking French food and one more hour riffing on the guitar and (b) François increases his time spent making French food by $\frac{4}{3}$ of an hour and decreases his time spent producing guitar riffs by $\frac{4}{3}$ of an hour. The resulting output of Bjørn and François after the new allocation of time is shown in Table 4.3. This right-most column of this table shows that, after some specialization, the combined output of Bjørn and François increases: total production of food stays constant and total production of guitar riffs increases by $\frac{2}{3}$ of a unit.

Table 4.4 **Bjørn and François production and consumption after some specialization**						
	Bjørn			François		
	produc.	consum.	produc. − consum.	produc.	consum.	produc. − consum.
Guitar riffs	50	$40\frac{1}{3}$	$+9\frac{2}{3}$	$18\frac{2}{3}$	$28\frac{1}{3}$	$-9\frac{2}{3}$
French food	24	32	−8	32	24	+8

For Bjørn and François to both unambiguously benefit from specialization in production, they need to agree to meet and exchange some goods. Suppose this occurs and Bjørn and François decide to evenly split the gains from specialization. The columns marked "consum" in Table 4.4 show Bjørn's and François's consumption of guitar riffs and French food after specialization and exchange. These columns show that Bjørn and François are both better off after exchange and trade: they each consume the same amount of food and more guitar riffs compared to the case of autarky.

Note that even though Bjørn still produces both guitar riffs and food, on-net Bjørn sells guitar riffs to and buys French food from François. Bjørn produces 50 riffs but consumes only $40\frac{1}{3}$ riffs, selling the remaining $9\frac{2}{3}$ riffs to François in exchange for 8 units of food. If we switch to the language of trade, Bjørn is a net exporter of guitar riffs to François and a net importer of French food from François. Analogously, François is a net importer of guitar riffs and exporter of French food to Bjørn.

The fact that both Bjørn and François are better off after agreeing to exchange and trade is not some manufactured coincidence, but a necessity of the arrangement. Why? Because all trade and exchange is voluntary. Bjørn would not bother trading with François if he could enjoy higher living standards by not trading; and François would not bother trading with Bjørn if he could do better for himself in autarky.

The reason that specialization and exchange are beneficial in this example is that Bjørn and François have relatively different skills. If Bjørn works one more hour at guitar riffs and one less hour at food, he increases his riffs by 10 units at the expense of the production of 8 units of food. For Bjørn, one extra guitar riff "costs" $\frac{8}{10}$ of one unit of food. Economists denote these costs as "opportunity costs" because Bjørn's time spent working is fixed, so any time spent producing guitar riffs is time not spent producing French food. Restated, the "price" of one riff to Bjørn is 0.80 units of food.[2] Similarly, if François works one more hour at guitar riffs and one less hour at food, he increases his riffs by 7 units at the opportunity cost of 6 units of food. For François, the price of one riff is $\frac{6}{7} = 0.86$ units of food. Thus, Bjørn is the low-cost producer of guitar riffs, and since there are only two goods, François is the low-cost producer of French food. The example illustrates that total output can be increased (relative to autarky) if Bjørn and François specialize in production of the good in which they have the relatively low opportunity cost.

Notice that nothing has been said about countries. In this example we are simply describing exchange between two guys named Bjørn and François. They could live next door to each other in Madison, Wisconsin. The specialization and exchange described in this example occurs between individuals living in the city, state, province, and country every day. Typically, any one person doesn't grow his own food, and repair his car, and build his home and furniture, and dye his clothes, etc. We each work full-time in an industry where we have a comparative advantage and produce quite specialized goods;

[2] Eight units of food buys 10 guitar riffs, so 0.8 units of food buys 1 guitar riff. Thus the price of guitar riffs in units of food is 0.8.

in a marketplace we exchange our specialized good for an entire basket of goods produced by many other people; and the process of specialization and exchange in the market increases total output (relative to autarky) and makes us all better off. Every day, I (Morris Davis) am a net exporter of economics knowledge and a net importer of everything else, and I believe that arrangement to be roughly efficient.[3]

So, what makes the topic of "international trade" special? Nothing really. The scenario of the previous section can be directly applied to the study of trade between countries: simply relabel Bjørn as "Norway" and François as "France." International trade is only different from the process of exchange that characterizes many economic interactions (both within and across countries) due to artificial and arbitrary lines that divide countries. In a given country, labor is typically freely mobile and all agents use the same unit of exchange (currency). In specific models of international trade, labor cannot easily migrate across countries, and the name and color of the unit of exchange (money) varies from country to country. But aside from transportation costs and taxes/tariffs, those seem to be the extent of the differences.

4.2 Current and Capital Accounts

In the example of Bjørn and François, I assumed that the value of all the guitar riffs that Bjørn exported to François was equal to the value of all the French food that François exported to Bjørn. This is a case of goods-for-goods trade: Neither Bjørn nor François walked away from the exchange with a "trade deficit."

---

[3] I will export more guitar riffs if the market price ever turns positive.

A trade deficit occurs after exchange when one party receives, on-net, goods and services worth more than the other country receives in goods and services in return. In such a case, the party that receives the more valuable shipment of goods and services writes a note promising to pay the remaining balance at some point in the future. The party receiving this note thus accepts a financial asset in exchange for goods and services delivered today. A trade deficit occurs in any situation in which goods and services are exchanged, at least in part, for financial assets.

A very stylized example of this is as follows. Exporters from China deliver TVs to the United States and accept dollars in return, and exporters from the United States deliver (say) software to China and accept – for simplicity – dollars in return. If the United States runs a trade deficit, Chinese citizens will receive more dollars from US purchasers of TVs than it spends on software. On-net, China will have traded goods and services (TVs) for financial assets (dollars). Dollars are financial assets to the Chinese because they can be used to purchase goods and services from US makers at any time. Similarly, the dollars that the Chinese hold are liabilities to US residents, since dollars that the Chinese hold can be used to claim output produced by US firms and workers.

This leads to an important accounting identity: the current account and the capital account must sum to zero:

$$\text{Current account} + \text{Capital account} = 0. \qquad (4.1)$$

The current account denotes the value of exports to foreigners less the value of imports from foreigners. The capital account denotes changes to the claims on US assets held by foreigners less changes to the claims on foreign assets held by US residents. To understand why this equation is an identity, consider the following intuition: suppose person x sells goods and assets to person y and they agree on a sale price of $100. The fact that there was a sale implies that person x received some combination of goods and assets worth $100 from person y in return. The value of goods and assets sold is equal to the value of goods and assets purchased, which delivers the accounting identity of equation (4.1).

4.3 Data on Current and Capital Accounts

Recall in Chapter 1 that we defined gross domestic product (GDP) as the sum of consumption, investment, government spending, and net exports. Net exports are defined as the nominal value of exports less the nominal value of imports. When net exports are zero, the dollar value of exports is equal to the dollar value of imports, and goods and services are exchanged only for goods and services. When net exports are greater than zero, the domestic country (say the US) is running a trade surplus, a situation in which US producers are, on-net, accepting foreign assets in exchange for goods and services produced today. When net exports are less than zero, the US is running a trade deficit, a situation in which foreign producers are, on-net, accepting US assets in exchange for goods and services produced today.

Data from Table 1.1.5 of the National Income and Product Accounts (NIPA), published by the Bureau of Economic Analysis (BEA), lists some basic facts about US exports and imports.[4] According to data

---

[4] The NIPA are available for free download at the BEA's website, www.bea.gov. Click on the "Gross Domestic Product (GDP)" link, then click on the "Interactive Tables: GDP and the National Income and Product Account (NIPA) Historical Tables" link, and then click on the "List of All NIPA Tables" link. Chapter 1 includes a detailed description of all the NIPA data.

Figure 4.1 Net exports, exports, and imports as a percentage of nominal GDP, 1929–2007

in this table, in 2007 the US exported $1,662.4 billion of goods and services and imported $2,370.2 billion of goods and services, such that net exports in 2007 was −$707.8 billion. Thus, the NIPA data suggest that, in 2007, US residents received about $700 billion more in goods and services from foreigners than foreigners received from US residents, and foreigners acquired about $700 billion more of US assets than foreign assets acquired by US residents.

Figure 4.1 shows the US trade balance and its components, as a percentage of GDP, for the entire period over which NIPA data are available, 1929–2007. Generally speaking, from 1929 through the mid-1970s, both exports (dotted line) and imports (long-dash line) were both roughly equal to 4 or 5 percent of GDP, and the US ran essentially no trade surpluses or deficits (solid line). Since the mid-1970s, both exports and imports as a percent of GDP have increased, and the US has run an increasing trade deficit. By 2007, the trade deficit accounted for −5.1 percent of total GDP. Table 4.5 shows US

Table 4.5 **US exports and imports of goods in $ millions in 2007 by major region**

	Exports	Imports	Net exports (goods)
Europe	$280,845	$411,179	−$130,334
Canada	$249,712	$320,323	−$70,611
Latin America	$243,063	$348,378	−$105,316
Asia and Pacific	$308,248	$718,562	−$410,314
Middle East	$43,646	$77,405	−$33,759
Africa	$22,966	$92,005	−$69,039
Total	$1,148,481	$1,967,853	−$819,373

exports and imports of goods (exclusive of services), by continent, in 2007. This table shows that the US both exported goods to and imported goods from all places, but on-net in 2007 the US imported goods from every major geographic region.[5]

4.4 Trade of Goods for Assets

Assets are claims to consumption at a future date. For example, you can withdraw money in your bank account at any time to buy consumption at any point in the future. Thus, the money in your bank account, which is a financial asset, gives you a claim to consumption in the future. This implies the running of a trade deficit – the trading of goods for assets – is equivalent to the purchasing of consumption today in exchange for consumption delivered in the future.

---

[5] The data in this table are from Table 2a, US Trade in Goods, of the International Economic Accounts of the BEA. To access this data, go to the BEA's website, www.bea.gov, click on the "Balance of Payments" link, then click on the "Interactive Tables: Detailed Estimates" link, and then click on the "Table 2a. U.S. Trade in Goods" link.

Table 4.6 **North and South production possibilities of tons of food**		
	North	South
Apr.–Sep.	100	20
Oct.–Mar.	20	100

One question that comes up – often – is why residents of the United States would find it in their best interest to run a trade deficit and sell future consumption (assets) to finance current consumption. It turns out that we can use the intuition of comparative advantage and the insight that assets are claims to future consumption to explain why a country might run a trade deficit.

Let's start with an example where the trade of goods for assets seems like an obvious way to increase the overall standard of living. Suppose there are two growing regions, North and South. Farmers in the North grow a lot of food from April to September but not much food from October to March. Conversely, farmers in the South grow a lot of food from October to March, but not much food from April to September. The production schedule for food for farmers in the North and South as a function of the calendar year is shown in Table 4.6. A key assumption we will make is that food is not storable. Without trade, residents in each region eat a lot of food in one season and do not eat much food at all in the other season.

Under standard assumptions about the marginal utility of food, residents in both regions would prefer an equal consumption of food in both seasons. Trade between regions provides both sets of residents with this opportunity. One possible allocation after trade occurs is shown in Table 4.7. In this allocation, the consumption of food is even in both regions throughout the year; the North exports food from April to September and imports food from October to March;

Table 4.7 **North and South production and consumption after trade**

	North			South		
	produc.	consum.	produc. − consum.	produc.	consum.	produc. − consum.
Apr.–Sep.	100	60	+40	20	60	−40
Oct.–Mar.	20	60	−40	100	60	+40

the South imports food from April to September and exports from October to March; and, no food is wasted. From April to September, the North is exchanging food for a written promise to deliver food in the future. This written promise is a financial asset, since it is a piece of paper that will be exchanged for future goods and services – in this case food over the October to March period. Thus, in this simple example, trade makes the consumption of food independent of the growing season and illustrates the potential for benefits when goods are exchanged for assets.

The fundamental reason that trade is beneficial between regions is that the implicit price of storage differs between the two regions in each season. As mentioned earlier, food is not storable, so there is no "price" for storage since storage is not an option. However, we can ask how much residents in each region would be willing to pay for storage if a storage technology existed. In the April to September period, residents in the North would be willing to forego many units of food today for a storage technology that provided for some food in the October to March season. If there existed a storage technology that paid a rate of interest, residents of the North might be willing to accept a negative rate of interest just to have access to the storage technology. Conversely, residents in the South would not be willing to pay much at all for storage in the April to September period, since they would prefer to consume more this season and less in the October to March season. If there existed a storage technology that paid a rate of interest, residents in the South would need a very large rate of interest to forego one unit of food during the April to September season. Because the required rate of interest on the storage technology (if one were to exist) differs across the two regions during the April to September (and, by extension, the October to March seasons when roles are reversed), opportunities for trade of goods for assets exist and make residents of both regions better off.

To add additional insight, let's return to our buddies Bjørn and François. Suppose Bjørn and François no longer make guitar licks and French food, but make two goods called "consumption today" and "future consumption." The production possibilities for Bjørn and François for consumption today and future consumption are shown in Table 4.8 below. The table also shows the allocation if Bjørn and François live in autarky, each spending 4 hours per day making consumption today, denoted C_t and future consumption, denoted C_{t+1}. Table 4.9 shows what happens if Bjørn and François specialize slightly, with Bjørn making more C_t and less C_{t+1} and François conversely specializing in making more C_{t+1} and less C_t. With specialization, world output of C_t does not change and is higher for C_{t+1} in Table 4.9 than in Table 4.8.

Table 4.10 shows the allocation of consumption today and consumption tomorrow to Bjørn and François after they specialize somewhat in production and trade, with Bjørn and François agreeing to split the gains from trade. Notice that trade makes both Bjørn and François better off in the future, in the sense that both increase their levels of future consumption relative to what they would have received in autarky.

Table 4.8 Bjørn and François production: autarky

	Bjørn			François			Total
	Output per hour	Hours	Total	Output per hour	Hours	Total	Total
C_t	20	4	80	10	4	40	120
C_{t+1}	21	4	84	11	4	44	128

Table 4.9 Bjørn and François production: some specialization

	Bjørn			François			Total
	Output per hour	Hours	Total	Output per hour	Hours	Total	Total
C_t	20	5	100	10	2	20	120
C_{t+1}	21	3	63	11	6	66	129

Table 4.10 Bjørn and François production and consumption after some specialization

	Bjørn			François		
	Produc.	Consum.	Produc. − consum.	Produc.	Consum.	Produc. − consum.
C_t	100	80	+20	20	40	−20
C_{t+1}	63	$84\frac{1}{2}$	$-21\frac{1}{2}$	66	$44\frac{1}{2}$	$+21\frac{1}{2}$

If one were to ignore the benefits of trade that will accrue to future consumption, François would appear to be a profligate spender, since he will be consuming 40 units today – double his current production – and selling off assets to finance this consumption. When viewed only from the current period, and not taking into account the full time-series path of consumption today and future consumption, it appears that François is selling off his future to enjoy consumption today. This interpretation of François's trade balance is dangerously incorrect. It is true that once period $t + 1$ arrives, François will ship $21\frac{1}{2}$ units of consumption to Bjørn – this is the payment that Bjørn demands for shipping 20 units of consumption to François in period t – however, even after the shipment, consumption at $t + 1$ for François will be higher than it would have been in the case of autarky, i.e. in the case where François and Bjørn do not specialize and trade.

The reason that Bjørn and François can have gains from trade is that they have different opportunity costs of the production of consumption today relative to future consumption. Since Bjørn's time spent working is fixed, for every 20 units of C_t that Bjørn produces, he foregoes 21 units of C_{t+1}. Thus for one extra unit of C_t Bjørn must forego 1.05 ($= 21/20$) units of C_{t+1}. In comparison, François must forego 1.10 ($= 11/10$) units of future consumption for an extra unit of consumption today. The reason that trade makes both Bjørn and François better off is that they can each specialize in making the good in which they have a comparative cost advantage: Bjørn specializes in producing C_t (since he has the lower opportunity cost of producing that good) and François specializes in producing C_{t+1}, since he is the relatively low-cost producer of future consumption.

The opportunity cost – price – of consumption today relative to consumption tomorrow is the interest rate on assets. To see this, we can study budget constraints. In the case of French food and guitar riffs, suppose Bjørn can buy French food f at price p_f and guitar riffs g at price p_g. Given a lifetime income denoted (for reasons to be made clear soon) as $(1 + r)\, y$, Bjørn's budget constraint is:

$$(1 + r)\, y = p_f * f + p_g * g. \tag{4.2}$$

Now suppose that instead of buying guitar riffs and French food, Bjørn uses income today y to buy consumption today C_t and future consumption C_{t+1}. Any income not spent on consumption today earns a rate of interest $1 + r$, financing future consumption:

$$C_{t+1} = (1 + r)(y - C_t).$$

This can be rewritten to have a similar form as the budget constraint for guitar riffs and French food:

$$(1 + r)y = (1 + r) * C_t + C_{t+1}. \qquad (4.3)$$

Now compare the budget constraints (4.2) and (4.3). Equation (4.2) shows that the price of French food relative to guitar riffs is p_f/p_g. Analogously, equation (4.3) shows that the price of current consumption C_t relative to future consumption C_{t+1} is $(1 + r)$.

In summary, any time that countries have different interest rates on their assets, there are gains to be had from trade. Relative to the allocation under autarky, the country with the ex-ante higher interest rate will, relative to autarky, (a) increase its current consumption after trade; (b) run a trade deficit and sell off some of its assets to finance this consumption; and (c) deliver consumption in the future to its trading partner.

In the case of trade between the US and China, say, the application of theory to the data is not so clear-cut. The US has a large trade deficit with China, meaning that US residents are receiving consumption today and promising the Chinese consumption in the future. For this to be consistent with the theory, interest rates must be higher in the US than in China. However, because China is a developing country, interest rates should be higher in China than in the US.[6] Thus, the theory presented so far predicts that the US should run a big trade surplus with China. As of right now, economists do not have a widely accepted explanation for the pattern of trade flows with China, but this is an active area of research.

---

[6] The rate of return on new investment in China should be high because China does not have enough capital given the size of its labor force (this is the definition of an underdeveloped country). See Chapter 2 for more of an explanation.

4.5 Factor Prices and Trade

In Chapter 2, we assumed that a typical firm in the US economy produced output according to a Cobb–Douglas production function, with technology z_t, capital K_t, and labor L_t as inputs:[7]

$$Y_t = z_t K_t^\alpha L_t^{1-\alpha}, 0 < \alpha < 1.$$

Technology is assumed to be freely available to all firms. When firms maximize profits, they set the marginal benefit of each of the costly inputs, capital and labor, equal to the marginal cost:

$$
\begin{aligned}
w_t &= (1-\alpha)\, z_t\, K_t^\alpha\, L_t^{-\alpha} \\
r_t &= \quad \alpha \quad z_t\, K_t^{\alpha-1}\, L_t^{1-\alpha}.
\end{aligned}
\tag{4.4}
$$

The marginal cost of an additional unit of labor is the wage rate, w_t, and the marginal cost of an additional unit of capital is the rental rate on capital, r_t. These marginal costs are equated to marginal benefits, which are simply the marginal products. Equation (4.4) shows that in a closed economy – an economy that does not trade with other economies – the wage rate and rental rate are a function of the level of technology and the domestic stocks of capital and labor.

Now suppose that the country starts trading with the rest of the world as of time $t+1$. A typical assumption in trade is that capital is mobile across countries but that labor is not. If capital is mobile, then it must earn the same rate of return in every country. This means that after trade, $r_{t+1} = \bar{r}$ where $\bar{r}$ is the worldwide rate of return on capital.[8]

---

[7] See Chapter 2 for a more thorough discussion of growth and the rate of return on capital.

[8] I assume for simplicity that the worldwide rate of return on capital is not affected by the entry of this country into the set of countries that trade.

The question is – what happens to the wage rate on labor after a country starts to trade? The answer depends on whether or not the domestic rate of return on capital prior to trade is less or greater than the worldwide rate. Let's start with the assumption that the domestic rate of return prior to trade, r_t, is greater than the worldwide rate such that $r_t > r_{t+1} = \bar{r}$. Suppose that the marginal cost of capital is assumed to equal the marginal benefit both before and after trade – that is, suppose the second line of equation (4.4) holds before and after trade. We can use this equation to determine what happens to the stock of capital after trade, assuming that the level of technology z_t and the labor input L_t do not change between periods t and $t+1$:

$$\frac{r_{t+1}}{r_t} = \left(\frac{K_{t+1}}{K_t}\right)^{\alpha-1} = \left(\frac{K_t}{K_{t+1}}\right)^{1-\alpha}. \tag{4.5}$$

Equation (4.5) shows that after trade the stock of capital used in production increases: since $r_{t+1} < r_t$ and $1 - \alpha > 0$, this implies $K_{t+1} > K_t$. Thus, when the domestic rate of return on capital is higher than the worldwide rate, trade leads to an inflow of capital from abroad. Capital flows into the domestic country from abroad for the obvious reason that the rate of return on capital in the domestic country is relatively high.

Assuming that the wage rate on labor is equal to the marginal product of labor both before and after trade, the inflow of new capital makes existing labor more productive. We can use the first line of equation (4.4) to show that the wage rate paid to labor rises between periods t and $t+1$ due to the capital inflows:

$$\frac{w_{t+1}}{w_t} = \left(\frac{K_{t+1}}{K_t}\right)^{\alpha}. \tag{4.6}$$

Thus, in situations when a country has a high rate of return on its capital and starts to trade with countries with lower rates of return on capital, and assuming that capital is mobile but labor is not, the theory predicts that after trade (a) the domestic rate of return on capital should fall and (b) the domestic wage rate on labor should rise. Of course, using exactly the same logic, it can be shown that in situations when a country has a low rate of return on its capital and starts to trade with countries that have a higher rate of return on capital, i.e. $r_t < \bar{r}$, then after trade the domestic rate of return on capital should increase and the domestic wage rate on labor should fall.

4.6 Topics in Exchange Rates

4.6.1 Covered Interest Parity

The idea that the rate of return on capital must be the same for all countries that trade is related to a condition called "covered interest parity." In covered interest parity, the current exchange rate and the contracted forward exchange rate must ensure that the effective rate of return on capital in the two countries is identical.

To make this idea clear, consider the example of the US and the UK. Suppose the effective annual risk-free rate of return on savings in UK banks is 5 percent, but US banks are offering risk-free certificates of deposit (CDs) paying 10 percent. Suppose also that the exchange rate is $2 = £1. If the one-year-ahead forward exchange rate is the same as the current exchange rate, then it is possible to make risk-free profits using the following trading strategy:

1. Borrow £1.00 from a UK bank with promise to repay £1.05 at end of year.
2. Convert £1.00 to $2.00 at the current exchange rate.
3. Lock in one year ahead forward exchange rate at £1.00 for $2.00.
4. Invest $2.00 in US for one year, receive $2.20 at end of year.

5. Convert $2.20 back to £1.10.

6. Pay back £1.05 to the UK bank and keep £0.05 as profit.

To eliminate the potential for risk-free profits earned using this kind of trading strategy, the one year ahead forward rate must be different than the current exchange rate. In the event that the risk-free rate required by residents of both countries is 5 percent, at the end of the year $2.20 must be converted to £1.05, such that steps 1–6 yield no profits. Therefore, the one year ahead forward rate must specify that £1 be convertible to $2.095, computed as $2.20/£1.05.

Generally speaking, forward rate contracts must specify that the dollar depreciates (appreciates) relative to foreign currencies whenever the risk-free rate of interest offered by US banks is higher (lower) than the risk-free rate offered in other countries. A formal way of expressing the covered interest parity equation, continuing to use the US and the UK as an example, is as follows:

$$(1 + i_\$) \, S_{\$/£} = (1 + i_£) \, F_{\$/£}, \tag{4.7}$$

where $i_\$$ is the annual rate of interest at US banks, $i_£$ is the annual rate of interest at UK banks, $S_{\$/£}$ is the "spot" (i.e. current) exchange rate of dollars per pound, and $F_{\$/£}$ is the contracted one year ahead forward exchange rate of dollars per pound. For example, inserting values from the earlier numerical example yields:

$$(1.10) \, 2.000 = (1.05) \, 2.095.$$

4.6.2 Purchasing Power Parity

The idea of "purchasing power parity" is something like the following: if goods are freely tradable and salable across borders, without taxes or transportation costs, then exchange rates should adjust until no arbitrage opportunities exist for people to buy and resell goods. For example, if Big Macs are costlessly and instantaneously transportable and salable, and there are no tariffs or taxes on Big Macs, then a Big Mac that sells for $2.00 in the US should sell for £1 in the UK if the exchange rate is £1 for $2.00.

We can use the example of the US and the UK to explicitly link purchasing power parity to covered interest parity and inflation rates. Suppose, as before, that the one-year risk-free rate offered at UK banks is 5 percent, the one-year risk-free rate offered at US banks is 10 percent, the exchange rate at the start of the year is $2.00 per £1, and the one-year forward exchange rate is $2.095 per £1 such that covered interest parity holds.

Now suppose that the price of one Big Mac is $2.00 in the US and £1.00 in the UK at the start of the year. If the inflation rate is 0 percent in the UK, the price of a Big Mac will be £1.00 at the end of the year. Assume also that the exchange rate at the end of the year is $2.095 per £1, such that the one-year-ahead forward exchange rate was an accurate predictor of the spot rate. If purchasing power parity holds, and Big Macs cannot be profitably shipped from the US to the UK or vice versa, then the price of a Big Mac in the US at the end of the year should be $2.095. This implies that the one-year rate of inflation on Big Macs in the US is 4.75 percent, computed as $100 * (\$2.095/\$2.00 - 1.00)$.

4.6.3 Fisher Equation

The interaction of covered interest parity, purchasing power parity, and inflation rates are intrinsically related to the Fisher equation, named after Irving Fisher (one of the early pioneers in the study of monetary economics).[9] The Fisher equation states that the nominal

---

[9] See the Wikipedia entry, http://en.wikipedia.org/wiki/Irving_Fisher, for more information on Irving Fisher.

rate of return paid to assets i is a function of the real rate of return r and the inflation rate π such that

$$(1 + i) = (1 + r)(1 + \pi). \tag{4.8}$$

If i, r, and π are sufficiently small, then this equation can be approximated as $i \approx r + \pi$.

We can apply the Fisher equation to our example from the previous section. In the case of the UK, the price of a Big Mac stays fixed at £1. Since there is no inflation, $\pi = 0$ and the nominal interest paid, 5 percent, is also the real rate of interest. In the United States, the price of a Big Mac increases from $2.00 to $2.095, such that $\pi = 0.0475$. We know the nominal interest rate is 10 percent, i.e. $i = 0.10$. Therefore the real rate of return on US assets solves

$$1.10 = (1 + r)(1.0475).$$

The value of r that is consistent with this equation is 0.05. In other words, the real rate of return on US assets is 5 percent, exactly the same real rate of return on assets that is paid in the UK. The fact that both countries pay the same real rate of return on assets is consistent with the idea that when capital is mobile, the real rate of return in all countries is identical, and differences in nominal rates of return are simply reflective of differences in inflation rates.

FURTHER READING

Of course the topics of international trade and international financial macroeconomics are much broader than the review given in this chapter. Here I just list a few points to think about.

- The benchmark model of trade is the Heckscher–Ohlin model. This model formalizes how differences in endowments across countries naturally lead to comparative advantages. An overview of the Heckscher–Ohlin model is available at http://en.wikipedia.org/wiki/Heckscher-ohlin_model.

- Due to the presence of taxes and transportation costs, and the input of non-internationally traded goods (such as land) in the production of final goods that people consume, the ratio of the price of consumption goods of two countries has typically not been found to equal the exchange rate. More information on purchasing power parity and the law of one price is available at http://en.wikipedia.org/wiki/Purchasing_power_parity.

H Homework

1 In the United States, one hour of labor can make 10 units of manufactures or 25 units of services. In Japan, one hour of labor can make 12 units of manufactures or 15 units of services.

   a. Assume Japan and the United States do not trade. Suppose the price of a manufacture in the United States is $100. What do you think the price of a unit of services is in the United States? Suppose the price of a manufactured good in Japan is ¥1,000. What do you think the price of a unit of services is in Japan?

   b. Should Japan and the United States trade? If not, explain your answer. If so, what should Japan export (and explain your answer)?

2 As in the previous question, assume that in the United States, one hour of labor can make 10 units of manufactures or 25 units of services. Now assume that in China, one hour of labor can make 6 units of manufactures or 5 units of services.

   Should the United States trade with China? If not, explain your answer. If so, what should China export (and explain your answer)?

3 Prior to trade, the annual real interest rate on assets in the US is 5 percent and the annual real interest rates in Europe is 3 percent.

   a. Prior to trade, what is the price of current consumption relative to future consumption in Europe and the US?
   b. Assume the US and Europe start to trade. Which will run a trade deficit and why?

4 Explain why the dollar may depreciate against the currencies of trade partners if the US has a higher rate of inflation than its trade partners and purchasing power parity holds.

5 On January 1, 2007, \$US1 can buy Japanese ¥100. The one-year real risk-free interest rate in both countries is 3 percent. The expected inflation rate in 2007 is 2.5 percent in the US and the inflation rate in Japan is expected to be 1.0 percent. Assuming that the Fisher equation, purchasing power parity, and covered interest parity hold, what is the forward exchange rate in ¥/\$ for January 1, 2008 when contracted on January 1, 2007?

5 | Business Cycles

O Objectives of this Chapter

We start the chapter by listing the dates of the business cycles experienced in the US after World War II as defined by a group of economists at the National Bureau of Economic Research (NBER).

We then review how economists define and measure cycles. We start with a discussion about how any series can be split into a trend and a cycle, and show that, by definition, different estimates of trend yield different estimates of cycles. We compare two different methods for detrending real GDP: a straight-line method and a more general method called the HP-Filter which encompasses the straight-line method. We discuss the derivation of the HP-Filter and how it is implemented and used in practice.

Next, we define four important properties of cyclical macroeconomic data: that is, properties of key macroeconomic data after the HP-Filter has been applied: (1) consumption is less volatile than GDP, (2) investment is more volatile than GDP, (3) hours worked is as volatile as GDP, and (4) hours worked, consumption, and investment are "pro-cyclical," meaning that when GDP is above trend, these other variables tend to be above trend as well.

At the end of the chapter, we briefly review the modern theory of business cycles, which suggests that business cycles arise when optimizing firms and households respond to fluctuations in the level of technology. Since the level of technology is, on average, increasing over time, the modern theory of business cycles is fundamentally linked to the theory of growth. Specifically, business cycles arise because the level of technology does not increase at exactly the same rate in each period, but rather displays cyclical patterns around a relatively fixed rate of growth.

5.1 Business Cycle Dates

A group of economists at the NBER label the periods when the economy is in "recession" and when the economy is in "expansion." Basically, and this is not quite a rule, the NBER economists label the economy as being in a recession when the growth rate of real GDP is negative for two consecutive quarters. In other words, a recession is associated with a decrease in the level of real output. The economy is expanding otherwise.

On the NBER's main business cycle page, www.nber.org/cycles/cyclesmain.html, a list of contraction and expansion dates for the US economy is presented. The quarterly reference dates starting in 1945, along with duration data (in months) are listed in Table 5.1. Figure 5.1 graphs the quarterly change in the natural log of real GDP over the 1949:1–2007:4 period. The shaded gray areas in this graph indicate the NBER recession dates that are listed in Table 5.1. Note that the change in the natural log of real GDP is approximately equal to the growth rate of real GDP: Defining y_t as real GDP in period t,[1] then

$$\ln(y_t) - \ln(y_{t-1})$$
$$= \ln\left(\frac{y_t}{y_{t-1}}\right) = \ln\left(1 + \frac{y_t - y_{t-1}}{y_{t-1}}\right) \approx \frac{y_t - y_{t-1}}{y_{t-1}}.$$

5.2 Trends and Cycles

Although the NBER labels are helpful, macroeconomists have also developed formal procedures for defining business cycles and studying the cyclical properties of major macroeconomic variables.

[1] See the appendix for a review.

Table 5.1 NBER business cycle dates

Dates		Duration (Months)			
Peak	Trough	Contraction*	Expansion**	Trough-Trough+	Peak-Peak++
1948:Q4	1949:Q4	11	37	48	45
1953:Q2	1954:Q2	10	45	55	56
1957:Q3	1958:Q2	8	39	47	49
1960:Q2	1961:Q1	10	24	34	32
1969:Q4	1970:Q4	11	106	117	116
1973:Q4	1975:Q1	16	36	52	47
1980:Q1	1980:Q3	6	58	64	74
1981:Q3	1982:Q4	16	12	28	18
1990:Q3	1991:Q1	8	92	100	108
2001:Q1	2001:Q4	8	120	128	128

* Months from peak to trough.
** Months from previous trough to this peak.
+ Months elapsed, trough from previous trough.
++ Months elapsed, trough from previous trough.

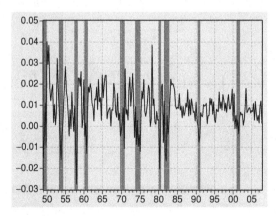

Figure 5.1 Quarterly change in log real GDP and dates of NBER contractions, 1949:1–2007:4

The reason economists study business cycles, separately from (say) growth, is that major macroeconomic variables have very different long-run trends than cyclical patterns. On p. 1 of their paper, Hodrick and Prescott (the developers of the HP-Filter, discussed later) provide some background on the study and measurement of business cycles:[2]

As Lucas (1981)[3] has emphasized, aggregate economic variables in capitalist economies experience repeated fluctuations about their long-term growth paths. Prior to Keynes' *General Theory*, the study of these rapid fluctuations, combined with the attempt to reconcile the observations with an equilibrium theory, was regarded as the main outstanding challenge of economic research . . .

The thesis of this paper is that the search for an equilibrium model of the business cycle is only beginning and that studying the comovements of aggregate economic variables using an efficient, easily replicable technique that incorporates our prior knowledge about the economy will provide insights into the features of the economy that an equilibrium theory should incorporate.

To study the fluctuations of "aggregate economic variables" around their trends or "long-term growth paths" requires a formal procedure to divide any variable into two components: a trend and a deviation from trend called the "cycle." A decomposition of a variable into its trend and cycle components is required to identify the cyclical variation of any variable. As an example, consider the case of real GDP. The natural log of quarterly real GDP is graphed in Figure 5.2. Given the data in this figure, what is the trend of log real GDP and what is the cycle?

---

[2] See R. Hodrick and E. Prescott, 1997, "Postwar US Business Cycles: An Empirical Investigation," *Journal of Money, Credit, and Banking*, vol. 29, pp. 1–16.

[3] See R. E. Lucas, Jr., 1981, *Studies in Business Cycle Theory*, Cambridge, MA: MIT Press.

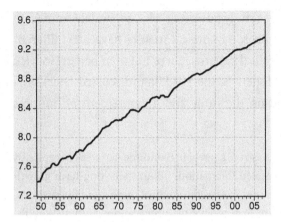

Figure 5.2 Log real GDP, 1949:1–2007:4

One "trend–cycle decomposition" of log real GDP plots a straight line through the series. In this decomposition, the straight line is the trend and the deviations from the straight line are the cycle. Define trend log real GDP as $\ln\left(y_t^*\right)$. A straight-line trend for log real GDP imposes that the slope of the line, which is equal to $\ln\left(y_t^*\right) - \ln\left(y_{t-1}^*\right)$, is a constant. Call this constant g: with a straight-line trend through log real GDP, the trend rate of growth of real GDP is fixed over time at $100 * g$ percent per year, since

$$\ln\left(y_t^*\right) - \ln\left(y_{t-1}^*\right) \approx \frac{y_t^* - y_{t-1}^*}{y_{t-1}^*} = g.$$

But is the assumption of constant trend growth of real GDP implied by a straight-line trend the best possible trend (according to some criterion)? Or should we allow the possibility of some other trend – perhaps a trend where the trend rate of growth of real GDP can change over time? Figure 5.3 shows two possible series for quarterly trend log real GDP. The dotted line shows a straight-line trend. The solid line shows a trend computed using the "HP-Filter," which we discuss in a moment. The solid line is more volatile than the dotted straight line,

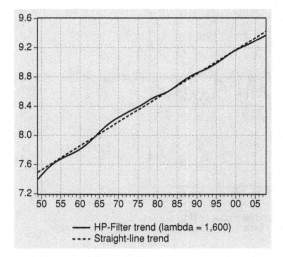

Figure 5.3 Trend log real GDP, trend computed using the HP-Filter and a straight line, 1949:1–2007:4

by definition: after all, a straight line is a straight line! Given these two possible definitions of trend log real GDP, Figure 5.4 shows the cycles, defined as the log of quarterly real GDP less its trend. In both cases, in each period the cycle (multiplied by 100) represents the percentage deviation of real GDP from its trend, since (using the same math as before)

$$\ln(y_t) - \ln(y_t^*) \approx \frac{y_t - y_t^*}{y_t^*}. \tag{5.1}$$

The dotted line shows the cycle when the straight-line trend is imposed and the solid line shows the cycle when the HP-Filter trend is imposed.

The cycle associated with the straight-line trend, the dotted line, has the undesirable feature that its average value is non-zero for long stretches of time: for example, the cycle is almost always below zero over the 1949–65 and 1990–2007 periods. Roughly speaking, economists (and statisticians) define a cyclical variable as a variable with two related properties: (1) the average value of the variable is

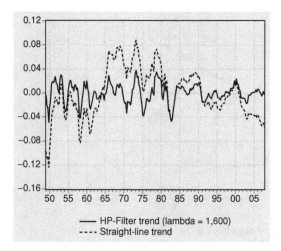

Figure 5.4 Log real GDP less trend, trend computed using the HP-Filter and a straight line, 1949:1–2007:4

approximately equal to zero in any sub-sample of the data of reasonable length; and (2) the variable crosses zero (turns from positive to negative and vice versa) at a relatively frequent pace. Based on these criteria, the cycle generated from a straight-line trend through log real GDP is not very "cyclical." In contrast, the cycle based on the HP-Filter trend, the solid line, appears to have both properties of a cycle: the average value is approximately zero in any sub-sample of reasonable length and the cycle crosses zero multiple times.

One reason the cycle based on the straight-line trend has undesirable properties is that the trend rate of growth of real GDP appears to change over time. For example, average real GDP growth fell by about 0.8 percentage points in 1973, from 3.8 percent per year over the 1947–73 period to 3.0 percent per year after 1973 (as discussed in Chapter 1). A straight-line trend through log real GDP averages through these different growth rates, producing a cycle with an average value that differs significantly from zero for large portions of the sample.

Given the knowledge that the growth rate of real GDP slowed sharply in 1973 it seems that, at a minimum, a straight-line-based trend should include at least two different segments: one from 1949–73 and another from 1973–2007 (with a lower growth rate). However, once we admit that a reasonable trend allows the trend rate of GDP growth to change at least once, then we might consider a trend where the rate of growth of the trend could possibly change in every period, albeit slowly or by small amounts. One procedure to compute trends that allows for a changing rate of growth is the Hodrick–Prescott Filter (HP-Filter). Continuing with the example of log real GDP, the HP-Filter computes the trend to log real GDP, $\ln(y_t^*)$, in each period to minimize the following expression

$$\sum_{t=1}^{T}\left[\ln(y_t) - \ln(y_t^*)\right]^2 + \lambda \sum_{t=2}^{T-1}\left[\Delta\ln(y_{t+1}^*) - \Delta\ln(y_t^*)\right]^2, \quad (5.2)$$

where $\Delta\ln(y_t^*) \equiv \ln(y_t^*) - \ln(y_{t-1}^*)$. λ is called the "smoothing parameter" and it determines the relative importance of (a) deviations of the series from trend and (b) changes to changes in the trend in the minimization of the above function. For example, if $\lambda = 0$, then changes to the change in trend are unimportant to the minimization criteria, and the HP-Filter sets log real GDP equal to trend log real GDP in every period, such that $\ln(y_t) = \ln(y_t^*)$. As $\lambda \to \infty$, the HP-Filter forces the change in trend log real GDP to be a constant, such that $\Delta\ln(y_{t+1}^*) = \Delta\ln(y_t^*) = g$. In this case, the HP-Filter produces the dotted straight line for trend log real GDP shown in Figure 5.3.

In modern studies of business cycles, typically researchers set $\lambda = 1,600$ in the case of quarterly data and $\lambda = 100$ for annual data. Under certain conditions, the square root of λ is equal to the ratio of the standard deviation of the cycle, $\ln{(y_t)} - \ln{(y_t^*)}$, to the standard deviation of changes to the change in trend (i.e. changes to the growth rate of trend real GDP), $\Delta \ln{(y_t^*)} - \Delta \ln{(y_{t-1}^*)}$.[4] On p. 4 of their paper, Hodrick and Prescott explain their choice of $\lambda = 1{,}600$ for quarterly data:[5] "Our prior view is that a 5 percent cyclical component is moderately large, as is a one-eighth of 1 percent change in the growth rate in a quarter. This led us to select $\sqrt{\lambda} = 5/(\frac{1}{8}) = 40$ or $\lambda = 1{,}600$ as a value for the smoothing parameter."

Note that if a moderately large quarterly change in the growth rate of trend is $\frac{1}{8}$ of 1 percent, then a moderately large annual change in the growth rate of trend could be $\frac{4}{8} = \frac{1}{2}$ of 1 percent, implying $\sqrt{\lambda} = 5/(\frac{1}{2}) = 10$ or $\lambda = 100$ for annual data.

The solid line shown for trend quarterly real GDP in Figure 5.3 and the cycle (deviation from trend) for log quarterly real GDP in Figure 5.4 are computed with $\lambda = 1{,}600$.[6] At $\lambda = 1{,}600$, the HP-Filter assigns a one-unit change in the change in the growth rate of trend real GDP, $\Delta \ln{(y_{t+1}^*)} - \Delta \ln{(y_t^*)}$, the same "penalty" as a 1,600-unit value for the percentage deviation of real GDP from its trend, $[\ln{(y_t)} - \ln{(y_t^*)}]$. For this reason, at $\lambda = 1{,}600$, the HP-Filter allows the growth rate of trend real GDP to change over time, but does not allow the growth rate of trend log real GDP to change by very much in any given period.[7]

---

[4] We define the concept of standard deviation later in this chapter.

[5] See Hodrick and Prescott, "Postwar US Business Cycles."

[6] In chapter 1, where I plot annual detrended log real GDP along with annual detrended log real consumption (Figures 1.5 and 1.6) and annual detrended log real investment (Figure 1.8), all variables have been detrended using the HP-Filter with $\lambda = 100$.

[7] If we were to exclusively work with the 1973:1–2007:4 sample, the cycle in log real GDP based on the HP-Filter with $\lambda = 1{,}600$ and the cycle in log real GDP arising from a straight-line trend (fitted to just this sample of data) are very similar. This

You may wonder how the HP-Filter is implemented in practice. The function defined in equation (5.2) is convex, and to minimize that function we set the derivatives of that function with respect to the trend variables equal to zero.[8] Consider the simplest useful case of four data periods, $t = 1, 2, 3, 4$, and relabel $\ln(y_t)$ as x_t and $\ln(y_t^*)$ as z_t. To solve for the HP-Filter trend, we take derivatives of

$$(x_1 - z_1)^2 + (x_2 - z_2)^2 + (x_3 - z_3)^2 + (x_4 - z_4)^2$$
$$+ \lambda\,(z_3 - 2z_2 + z_1)^2 + \lambda\,(z_4 - 2z_3 + z_2)^2$$

with respect to z_1, z_2, z_3, and z_4 and set each of these derivatives to zero. This gives us the following four equations (which you should check):

$$z_1: \quad 0 = -2\,(x_1 - z_1) + 2\lambda\,(z_3 - 2z_2 + z_1)$$
$$z_2: \quad 0 = -2\,(x_2 - z_2) - 4\lambda\,(z_3 - 2z_2 + z_1) + 2\lambda\,(z_4 - 2z_3 + z_2)$$
$$z_3: \quad 0 = -2\,(x_3 - z_3) + 2\lambda\,(z_3 - 2z_2 + z_1) - 4\lambda\,(z_4 - 2z_3 + z_2)$$
$$z_4: \quad 0 = -2\,(x_4 - z_4) \qquad\qquad\qquad + 2\lambda\,(z_4 - 2z_3 + z_2)$$

After dividing by 2 and rearranging terms, these equations can be expressed in matrix algebra form as

$$
\begin{bmatrix} x_1 \\ x_2 \\ x_3 \\ x_4 \end{bmatrix}
=
\begin{bmatrix}
\lambda + 1 & -2\lambda & \lambda & 0 \\
-2\lambda & 5\lambda + 1 & -4\lambda & \lambda \\
\lambda & -4\lambda & 5\lambda + 1 & -2\lambda \\
0 & \lambda & -2\lambda & \lambda + 1
\end{bmatrix}
\begin{bmatrix} z_1 \\ z_2 \\ z_3 \\ z_4 \end{bmatrix},
$$

explains why, for simplicity, I run a straight-line trend through the 1973:1–2007:4 period in certain parts of this book.

[8] See the appendix for details.

which has the simple solution

$$
\begin{bmatrix} z_1 \\ z_2 \\ z_3 \\ z_4 \end{bmatrix} = \begin{bmatrix} \lambda+1 & -2\lambda & \lambda & 0 \\ -2\lambda & 5\lambda+1 & -4\lambda & \lambda \\ \lambda & -4\lambda & 5\lambda+1 & -2\lambda \\ 0 & \lambda & -2\lambda & \lambda+1 \end{bmatrix}^{-1} \begin{bmatrix} x_1 \\ x_2 \\ x_3 \\ x_4 \end{bmatrix}.
$$

Thus, running an HP-Filter requires one matrix inversion, an easy task given current computing power and software.[9]

5.3 Business Cycle Statistics

In this section, we document the cyclical properties of four major macroeconomic variables: GDP, consumption, investment, and hours worked. We start by considering Figures 5.5, 5.6, and 5.7. Figure 5.5 plots detrended log real consumption alongside detrended log real GDP; Figure 5.6 plots detrended log real investment alongside detrended log real GDP; and Figure 5.7 shows detrended real log GDP and detrended log hours worked together. In each graph, the shaded gray areas represent NBER recession dates. In every case, we HP-Filter the natural logarithm of each variable with $\lambda = 1,600$. Thus, the percentage deviation of the major macroeconomic variable from its HP-Filtered trend is plotted – see equation (5.1). All data are quarterly over the 1949:1–2007:4 period except for the hours-worked series which ends in 2007:3.

These figures illustrate four key features of business cycles:

• Consumption is less volatile (smoother) than GDP.
• Investment is more volatile than GDP.

---

[9] For example, the MINVERSE command in Microsoft Office Excel can be used to invert a matrix.

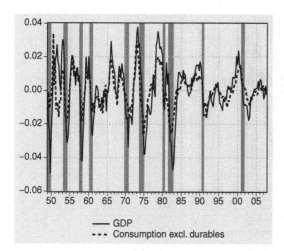

Figure 5.5 Detrended real GDP and detrended real consumption excl. durables, 1949:1–2007:4

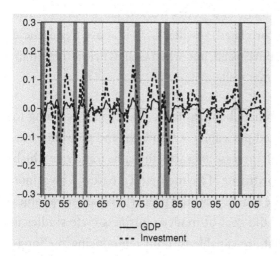

Figure 5.6 Detrended real GDP and detrended real investment, 1949:1–2007:4

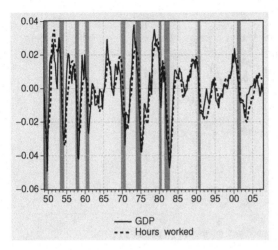

Figure 5.7 Detrended real GDP and detrended hours worked, 1949:1–2007:3

- Hours worked is about as volatile as GDP.
- Consumption, investment and hours worked are all pro-cyclical (meaning positively correlated) – when GDP is above trend, these variables tend to be above trend, and when GDP is below trend they tend to be below trend as well.

Notice the key differences between trend and cycle. According to Chapter 2, hours worked per capita is trendless, and consumption, investment, and GDP all increase at exactly the same trend rate which is determined by the growth rate of technological progress. This stands in quite a contrast to the four key cyclical properties of these variables just mentioned. Thus, the goal of modern business cycle studies is to produce models that are capable of both reproducing the long-run trends of these variables and matching the business cycle facts. Specifically, economists test the cyclical properties of models that are designed to be consistent with the long-term growth observations by seeing how accurately the models can match the cyclical standard deviation of GDP, consumption, investment, and hours worked, and how accurately they can match the cyclical correlations of GDP and consumption, GDP and investment, and GDP and hours worked.

To explain standard deviations and correlations, we have to start with the ideas of variance and covariance. The variance of a variable x_t, with $t = 1, \ldots, T$ observations and a sample average of $\bar{x}$, is computed as

$$\text{Var}\,(x) = \frac{\sum_{t=1}^{T} (x_t - \bar{x})^2}{T - 1}.$$

The variance measures the average of the square of a variable's deviation from its average. The standard deviation is the square root of the variance. Thus, the standard deviation gives an interpretation of the typical size of the deviation of a variable from its average value.

Table 5.2 reports standard deviations of the logged and HP-Filtered macro variables over the 1949:1–2007:4 period (1949:1–2007:3 in the case of hours worked). The estimates in this table provide empirical benchmarks for researchers developing quantitative models of the business cycle.[10] The table confirms and quantifies the evidence shown in Figures 5.5, 5.6, and 5.7. Column 2 of this table lists key statistics of business cycles: consumption (row b) is 62 percent as volatile as GDP (i.e. the standard deviation of logged and HP-Filtered real consumption is equal to 0.62 that of the standard deviation of logged and HP-Filtered real GDP); investment (row c) is 4.76 times more volatile than GDP; and hours worked (row d) is almost exactly as volatile as GDP.

---

[10] See, for example, T. Cooley and E. Prescott, 1995, "Economic Growth and Business Cycles," in *Frontiers of Business Cycle Research*, edited by Thomas F. Cooley, Princeton, NJ: Princeton University Press; or, M. A. Davis and J. Heathcote, 2005, "Housing and the Business Cycle," *International Economic Review*, vol. 46, pp. 751–784.

Table 5.2 Percentage standard deviations

Variable (x)	(1) % Standard Deviation*	(2) Relative % Std. Dev.**
(a) GDP	1.61	1.00
(b) Consumption	1.00	0.62
(c) Investment	7.64	4.76
(d) Hours worked	1.56	0.97

* Computed as 100 times the standard deviation of $\log(x_t) - \log(x_t^*)$ where x_t is the macroeconomic variable in question (GDP, consumption, investment, hours worked) and x_t^* is the HP-Filtered trend of that variable with $\lambda = 1,600$.
** Computed as the percentage standard deviation of the variable divided by the percentage standard deviation of GDP.

Continuing, the covariance of two variables x_t and y_t, with $t = 1, \ldots, T$ observations and sample averages of $\bar{x}$ and $\bar{y}$, respectively, is computed as[11]

$$\text{Cov}(x, y) = \frac{\sum_{t=1}^{T} (x_t - \bar{x})(y_t - \bar{y})}{T - 1}.$$

The covariance measures the comovement of two variables. If the covariance is larger than zero, this means that whenever x_t is above its average value, y_t tends to be above its average value. Likewise, if the covariance is less than zero, whenever x_t is above its average value, y_t tends to be below its average value. The correlation of x_t and y_t is just the rescaled covariance: it is equal to the covariance divided by the product of the standard deviation of x_t and the standard deviation of y_t. By definition, the correlation ranges between -1 and 1. If the

---

[11] The concept of covariance is also explained in Chapter 3.

Table 5.3 **Correlations**			
	(1)	(2)	(3)
		Correlations*	
Variable (x)	(GDP_t, x_{t-1})	(GDP_t, x_t)	(GDP_t, x_{t+1})
(a) GDP	0.84	1.00	0.84
(b) Consumption	0.77	0.79	0.62
(c) Investment	0.76	0.86	0.65
(d) Hours worked	0.64	0.83	0.88

* The correlation of the detrended logged variable x (GDP, consumption, investment, hours worked) at dates $t-1$, t, and $t+1$ with detrended logged GDP at date t.

correlation is positive, x_t and y_t are said to "move together" (i.e. be above their average value, on average, at the same time). It is useful to talk about correlations rather than covariances because correlations can be compared across pairs of variables, whereas covariances cannot.[12]

Note that x_t and y_t do not have to be two completely different variables. y_t can have the interpretation of being equal to x_t measured at a different date, for example y_t could be set to x_{t-1}. When we measure the correlation of x_t with one of its lags such as $y_t = x_{t-1}$ or one of its leads such as $y_t = x_{t+1}$ we are said to be measuring "autocorrelations" of x.

Table 5.3 shows the business cycle correlations of logged and HP-Filtered real GDP with its own leads and lags (row a), and with the quarterly leads and lags of detrended log consumption (row b),

[12] As an example, suppose the covariance between x_t and y_t is 0.1 and the covariance between x_t and z_t is 10.0. This does not mean that the correlation of x_t and y_t is greater than the correlation of x_t and z_t – if the standard deviation of z_t is much larger than the standard deviation of y_t, then the correlation of x_t and y_t might be larger than the correlation of x_t and z_t.

investment (row c), and hours worked (row d). Row (a) shows that GDP is positively correlated with its first lead and lag. Thus, deviations of GDP from trend are persistent – when GDP is above trend at time t, it tends to be above trend at time $t-1$ and $t+1$. Detrended log GDP is also positively correlated with detrended log consumption (row b column 2), investment (row c column 2), and hours worked (row d column 2). When GDP is above trend, it is highly likely that consumption, investment, and hours worked are also above trend – the correlation of these variables at time t with GDP at time t is 0.80 or above.

5.4 The Theory of Business Cycles

The goal of modern macroeconomic models is to explain the business cycle facts of the previous section using a tightly organized and internally consistent framework. A thoughtful framework simultaneously combines the ingredients of firm behavior and household behavior, and includes a well-specified definition of equilibrium. The essential ingredients of business cycle models are as follows:

1. Firms maximize profits by demanding capital and labor and supplying output (Chapter 2). Firms take the price of capital (r) and the price of labor (w) as given and outside their control.
2. Households maximize utility subject to their budget constraint by demanding output (to be split into consumption and savings) and supplying labor and capital (Chapter 3). Households take the price of capital (r) and the price of labor (w) as given and outside their control.
3. An equilibrium is a set of prices, r and w, such that firms maximize profits, households maximize utility, and markets clear: output

supplied by firms is equal to output demanded by households, and capital and labor demanded by firms is equal to capital and labor supplied by households.

A more advanced treatment of the theory of business cycles is not appropriate for this book. However, we might be able to gain some intuition for the theory if we review a few key ideas. First, recall that optimal consumption has the following solution

$$\frac{C_{t+1}}{C_t} = \beta \left(1 + \widehat{r}_{t+1}\right). \tag{5.3}$$

Suppose we are in a situation where we expect interest rates in period $t + 1$ to be relatively high. The equation describing optimal consumption also suggests that consumption in period $t + 1$ should also be high relative to consumption in period t.

But what would cause an increase in interest rates? Based on our theory of firm behavior from Chapter 2, we know that the marginal product of capital is

$$r_{t+1} = \alpha * z_{t+1} K_{t+1}^{\alpha-1} L_{t+1}^{1-\alpha}. \tag{5.4}$$

Now consider a surge in z_{t+1}, but hold capital and labor fixed. Two outcomes occur:

1. The marginal product of capital r_{t+1} increases. Since $\widehat{r}_{t+1}$ is linked to r_{t+1} via equation (2.16), the after-tax rate of return earned by households also increases.
2. Output increases. This is because output is equal to $z_{t+1} K_{t+1}^{\alpha} L_{t+1}^{1-\alpha}$, and z has increased while capital and labor have been held fixed. This increase in output in $t + 1$ is consistent with the increase in consumption. That is, consumption and output increase at the same time.

Summarizing, a temporary shock to technology can cause consumption, output, and interest rates to all increase at the same time. In fact, if we allow households to live much longer than two periods (say, live an infinite number of periods), then the model of household behavior we documented in the previous section can come very close, quantitatively, to matching the key business cycle facts – when realistic data-based fluctuations to technology (z_t) are used in simulations of the model.

With this in mind, we can view booms and busts of real GDP as just reflecting relatively high and low levels of technology. That is, technology increases at a relatively fixed rate over time, consistent with the long-run growth observations of Chapter 2; but the level of technology can persistently deviate from its growing trend, explaining the business cycle facts of this chapter. This insight is one reason that the 2004 Nobel Prize was awarded to Finn E. Kydland and Edward C. Prescott.[13]

FURTHER READING

- If you look closely at Figure 5.1, it appears that the variation of real GDP growth declined by quite a bit around 1985. By now, the reduction in the volatility of fluctuations of growth in real GDP is a well-documented phenomenon called "the great moderation."[14] The reduction in the volatility of GDP has not been

---

[13] See F. Kydland and E. Prescott, 1982, "Time to Build and Aggregate Fluctuations," *Econometrica*, vol. 50, pp. 1345–1370. Models continue to build on the framework of the original paper of Kydland and Prescott. A few recent examples of specification and calibration of models with a housing (or home-production) focus are P. Gomme and P. Rupert, 2007, "Theory, Measurement and Calibration of Macroeconomic Models," *Journal of Monetary Economics*, vol. 54, pp. 460–497 and Davis and Heathcote, "Housing and the Business Cycle."

[14] For an early paper documenting the reduction in the volatility of GDP, see C. Kim and C. Nelson, 1999, "Has the US Economy Become More Stable? A Bayesian

limited to the United States; a recent paper[15] suggests that the volatility of real GDP growth has significantly declined in 16 of 25 developed economies. In the US, for example, the standard deviation of changes to log real GDP, log real consumption, log real investment, and log hours worked all fell by 50 percent over the 1986–2007 period when compared to the 1949–85 period.

We do not know what accounts for the reduction in the volatility of GDP and the other macro aggregates; so far, there are three theories, none universally accepted.[16] The first is that changes in technology (like inventory management), coupled with financial innovation and deregulation (allowing better access to credit for households and firms), have enabled firms and households to better allocate risk and respond to shocks. The second theory is that better policy – specifically, monetary policy – has reduced the volatility of inflation and output. The third is that, worldwide, there has been good luck: shocks are simply smaller than they used to be, and thus the volatility of GDP and other macro aggregates has been reduced as a result.

With the advent of the "financial crisis" of 2008, it seems that the third explanation – good luck – may be the correct one. With another five years of data, we will know if the 1986–2007 period of relatively low volatility was a historical anomaly.

- Business reporting in newspapers often focuses on current events. For this reason, articles in the newspapers are sometimes helpful for

Approach Based on a Markov-Switching Model of the Business Cycle," *Review of Economics and Statistics*, vol. 81, pp. 608–16.

[15] See S. Cecchetti, A. Flores-Lagunes, and S. Krause, 2006, "Assessing the Sources of Changes in the Volatility of Real Growth," NBER Working Paper 11946, Cambridge, MA.

[16] See the speech by B. Bernanke, "Remarks by Governor Ben S. Bernanke at the Meetings of the Eastern Economic Association on the Great Moderation, Washington DC," 2004. The text of the speech is available at www.federalreserve.gov/boarddocs/speeches/2004/20040220/default.htm.

getting a feel for the current stage of the business cycle – for example, whether or not we are expanding or contracting.

Although newspapers have their place, I find that blogs can have more thoughtful discussion of the current events. Blog articles have some advantages over newspaper articles: bloggers have no word-count requirements, do not need to fetch multiple quotations from other industry experts, and do not have to worry that their story is accessible to all readers.

In the links below, I include some blogs (in alphabetical order of the author's last name) that I ask my students to look at for analysis of current economic news and events. Of course, I don't agree with every blogger or blog article, but I typically find the perspectives and analysis interesting. These blogs often have links to articles in other blogs, so over time you will probably build your own list of favorite bloggers.[17]

- "Macroblog" (David Altig)
  http://macroblog.typepad.com/macroblog
- "Econbrowser" (Menzie Chinn and James Hamilton)
  www.econbrowser.com
- New York Times "The Conscience of a Liberal" (Paul Krugman)
  http://krugman.blogs.nytimes.com
- Wall Street Journal "Real Time Economics" (Sudeep Reddy)
  http://blogs.wsj.com/economics
- "Global EconoMonitor" (Nouriel Roubini)
  www.rgemonitor.com/blog/roubini
- "Follow the Money" (Brad Setser)
  http://blogs.cfr.org/setser

[17] In addition to the following blogs about macroeconomics, I read "Richard's Real Estate and Urban Economics Blog," available at http://real-estate-and-urban.blogspot.com.

- "Economist's View" (Mark Thoma)
  http://economistsview.typepad.com
- "Calculated Risk: Finance and Economics" (Anonymous)
  http://calculatedrisk.blogspot.com
- "Angry Bear" (Anonymous)
  http://angrybear.blogspot.com

(H) Homework

1 Go to NIPA Table 1.1.6 and download annual real gross domestic product (line 1), real personal consumption expenditures (line 2), and real gross private domestic investment (line 6) over the 1949–2007 period. Take the natural log of each of these variables and then detrend each variable using the HP-Filter to each variable with parameter $\lambda = 100$.

In other words, for variable x_t, where x_t is either real GDP, real consumption, or real investment, compute the trend of $\ln(x_t)$ using the HP-Filter with $\lambda = 100$. Call the trend $\ln(x_t^*)$. Then compute $\ln(x_t) - \ln(x_t^*)$.

a. What are the standard deviations of the detrended variables over the 1949–2007 period? How do these estimates compare to those reported in Table 5.2?

b. What are the standard deviations of the detrended variables over the 1975–85 period and (separately) the 1985–2007 period?

To apply the HP-Filter in Microsoft Office Excel, you will need to download an Excel add-in. Kurt Annen has kindly made this add-in available to readers of this book: The file can be downloaded from the companion website for this book, www.cambridge.org/macro4mba.

2 The MELON ("MacroEconomics Laboratory ONline") project generates business cycle statistics produced by a modern business cycle model.[18] To enable access to this project, please go to the companion website for this book, www.cambridge.org/macro4mba, and follow the listed instructions. Upon gaining access to the MELON project, you should go to the site and click on the "Run the Business cycle model" link. Then, produce a run with the following information filled in:

Summary of parameter	Value
Value of T	200
Number of quarters for new capital	1
Fraction of total time spent in market work	0.25
Risk aversion parameter	3
Inventory–GDP ratio	0.25
Labor share of income	0.68
Permanent shock	0.70
Temporary shock	0.00

Compare the standard deviations and correlations of GDP, consumption, investment, and the labor input generated by the model to the statistics shown in the tables in this chapter. What do you find? In what dimensions does the model "fail" and "succeed"?

[18] For more information on the MELON project, see http://melon.uib.no/projects/melon.

6 | Monetary Policy

O   Objectives of this Chapter

This chapter describes the history and implementation of monetary policy in the United States. The first section provides a very brief overview of the history of central banking in the United States. This section concludes with a discussion of the stated objectives of the Federal Reserve System. Specifically, the "dual mandate" of monetary policy is discussed – the idea that the Federal Open Market Committee (FOMC) (which is one component of the Federal Reserve System) has been directed by Congress to set monetary policy with an eye towards the dual goals of full employment and stable prices.

In the second section of the chapter, we describe an approximation to the method by which the Federal Open Market Committee has implemented monetary policy to satisfy its dual mandate for the past 20 years. Specifically, we discuss the "Taylor rule" for monetary policy. The Taylor rule specifies that the FOMC sets the Federal Funds Rate – the overnight rate at which banks borrow reserves from each other – as a function of data on GDP (full employment) and inflation (stable prices). We compare the predicted Federal Funds Rate based on the Taylor rule to the actual Federal Funds Rate as set by the FOMC and show that the predictions of the Taylor rule imperfectly align with the data.

The third and final section of this chapter discusses the "quantity theory of money," which links growth in the stock of money to growth in real GDP and inflation. The chapter ends with a review of the historical relationship between growth in the stock of money and the inflation rate.

6.1 A Very Brief History of the Federal Reserve

The Federal Reserve System, the central banking system currently in place in the United States, was established in 1913 as a consequence of the Federal Reserve Act.[1] Prior to 1913, the US had twice experimented with limited central banking systems, from 1791–1811 and from 1816 to 1836. Between 1836 and 1913, the banking sector in the United States changed in some fundamental ways, but there was no central bank to speak of. The central bank was reestablished in 1913 after sizable financial panics due to bank runs were experienced in 1893 and 1907. These panics convinced many that a central banking authority might be a requirement for a stable financial system. Specifically, the central bank was designed "to function primarily as a reserve, a money-creator of last resort to prevent the downward spiral of withdrawal/withholding of funds which characterizes a monetary panic."[2] Ultimately, the Federal Reserve Act established this system.

The specifics of the governance of the Federal Reserve System changed from 1913 through 1950, but have essentially been constant since 1951. Currently, the Federal Reserve System consists of three entities: the Federal Reserve Board of Governors (commonly called the Federal Reserve Board), 12 Regional Federal Reserve Banks (one for each district),[3] and the FOMC. Together, the Board, the banks, and the FOMC have three responsibilities: to provide financial services, such as the processing of checks; to supervise banks, which

---

[1] Much of this material is drawn from three sources: The "History of the Federal Reserve," available at the Federal Reserve Board website at www.federalreserveeducation.org/fed101/history, "Understanding the Fed," available at the Federal Reserve Bank of Dallas website at www.dallasfed.org/fed/understand.cfm, and a publication from the Federal Reserve Bank of St. Louis called "In Plain English: Making Sense of the Federal Reserve," available at www.stls.frb.org/publications/pleng/PDF/PlainEnglish.pdf.

[2] This quotation is taken from the Wikipedia article "History of Central Banking in the United States," available at http://en.wikipedia.org/wiki/ History_of_central _banking_in_the_United_States. Interested readers should consult this article for additional content on this topic.

[3] The 12 Reserve Banks are in Boston, New York, Philadelphia, Cleveland, Richmond, Atlanta, Chicago, St. Louis, Minneapolis, Kansas City, Dallas, and San Francisco.

Table 6.1 **Chairmen of the Federal Reserve Board**	
Chairman	Date
Charles S. Hamlin	1914–1916
William P. G. Harding	1916–1922
Daniel R. Crissinger	1923–1927
Roy A. Young	1927–1930
Eugene Meyer	1930–1933
Eugene R. Black	1933–1934
Marriner S. Eccles	1934–1948
Thomas B. McCabe	1948–1951
William McChesney Martin, Jr.	1951–1970
Arthur F. Burns	1970–1978
G. William Miller	1978–1979
Paul A. Volcker	1979–1987
Alan Greenspan	1987–2006
Ben Bernanke	2006–

involves administering bank audits to verify that banks are properly managed to face the risks they assume; and to conduct monetary policy. Although the provision of financial services and bank supervision are important duties of the Federal Reserve System, in the rest of this chapter we focus on the third duty: the conduct of monetary policy.

The 12-member FOMC is responsible for the setting of monetary policy. There are eight permanent members of the FOMC and four temporary members. The eight permanent members of the FOMC include all seven members of the Federal Reserve Board and the president of the Federal Reserve Bank of New York. The four temporary members are rotating Federal Reserve Bank presidents who serve one-year terms. The chairman of the Federal Reserve Board is also the chairman of the FOMC. Since 1914, there have been 14 chairmen of the Federal Reserve Board: see Table 6.1 for a complete list.

Although the FOMC has at its disposal a suite of tools it can use to set monetary policy, its main policy tool is the setting of the Federal Funds Rate, the overnight rate at which banks can borrow bank reserves. Mechanically, the FOMC adjusts this rate by "open market operations," meaning it sets this rate by buying and selling US Treasuries in the open market. Specifically, if the FOMC wants to lower the Federal Funds Rate, it purchases US Treasuries from brokers or dealers and pays them by depositing reserves into their accounts. By exchanging Treasuries for reserves, the FOMC creates new reserves and increases the total supply of reserves in the market. Assuming the demand for reserves does not change, the increase in the supply of reserves implies (through standard supply and demand analysis) that the market-clearing interest rate on reserves falls. If the FOMC wants to increase the Federal Funds Rate, it sells US Treasuries to brokers and dealers and collects payment from their reserve accounts. This reduces the total amount of reserves in the economy, causing the market-clearing interest rate on reserves to increase.

So the natural next question is: how does the FOMC determine the appropriate Federal Funds Rate? Or, restated, what are the objectives of monetary policy? Frederic S. Mishkin outlined his views on the objectives of monetary policy – the "dual mandate" of the FOMC – in a speech he gave, while he was a member of the FOMC, at Bridgewater College, in Bridgewater, Virginia, on April 10, 2007:[4]

In a democratic society like our own, the ultimate purpose of the central bank is to promote the public good by pursuing a course of monetary policy that fosters economic prosperity and social welfare. In the United States, as in virtually every other country, the central bank has a more specific set of

---

[4] The title of the speech is "Monetary Policy and the Dual Mandate" and the full text is available at http://www.federalreserve.gov/newsevents/speech/mishkin20070410a.htm.

objectives that have been established by the government. This mandate was originally specified by the Federal Reserve Act of 1913 and was most recently clarified by an amendment to the Federal Reserve Act in 1977.

According to this legislation, the Federal Reserve's mandate is "to promote effectively the goals of maximum employment, stable prices, and moderate long-term interest rates." Because long-term interest rates can remain low only in a stable macroeconomic environment, these goals are often referred to as the dual mandate; that is, the Federal Reserve seeks to promote the two coequal objectives of maximum employment and price stability.

So, specifically, how does the FOMC set the Federal Funds rate to achieve the dual mandate of maximum employment and price stability? The answer, unfortunately, is that we're not really sure. The FOMC has never announced a predetermined rule that exactly guides how it sets or changes interest rates to achieve its objectives. Rather, the FOMC uses judgment or "discretion" in setting the Federal Funds rate. For this reason, the specific way that monetary policy and the Federal Funds rate have been set by the FOMC has varied over time.[5] In the next section, we study the practical implementation of monetary policy starting in 1987, the first year Alan Greenspan was chairman of the Federal Reserve Board.

6.2 The Taylor Rule

John Taylor at Stanford was the first to notice that, when Alan Greenspan became chairman of the Federal Reserve Board, monetary policy looked as though it had been (approximately) governed

---

[5] For example, Arthur Burns and Paul Volcker likely were not setting monetary policy using the same implicit rule; inflation increased during Burns's tenure, whereas inflation declined during Volcker's.

by the following equation:[6]

$$r_t^{ff} = \pi^* + \bar{r}^{ff} + \theta_1 \left[100.0 * \ln \left(GDP_t / GDP_t^* \right) \right]$$
$$+ \theta_2 \left(\pi_t - \pi^* \right). \quad (6.1)$$

Equation (6.1) is commonly called the "Taylor rule." To explain the variables of this equation:

- r_t^{ff} is the nominal Federal Funds rate, the overnight interest rate for bank reserves, expressed as an annual percent. For example, the average value of r_t^{ff} in 2007:Q4 was 4.50 percent.
- π_t is yearly (four-quarter) consumer price inflation, expressed as an annual percent as of period t. For example, the overall rate of consumer price inflation (excluding food and energy) that prevailed over the previous year in 2007:Q4 was 2.08 percent.
- GDP_t is real GDP and GDP_t^* is trend real GDP. $100.0 * \ln \left(GDP_t / GDP_t^* \right)$ is approximately equal to the percentage deviation of real GDP from trend. For example, I compute $100.0 * \ln \left(GDP_t / GDP_t^* \right)$ equal to -1.60 in 2007:Q4, meaning real GDP was 1.6 percent below trend in that quarter.
- π_t^* is the FOMC's target rate of consumer price inflation and $\bar{r}^{ff}$ is the inflation-adjusted Federal Funds rate, both in annual percent terms, when GDP is equal to its trend and inflation is equal to its target rate.

Notice that the Taylor rule has two arguments related to its dual mandate of maximum employment and price stability: deviations of output from its trend ($100.0 * \ln \left(GDP_t / GDP_t^* \right)$) and deviation of inflation from its desired rate ($\pi_t - \pi^*$). θ_1 and θ_2 are coefficients

---

[6] See J. Taylor, 1993, "Discretion Versus Policy Rules in Practice," *Carnegie-Rochester Series on Public Policy*, vol. 39, pp. 195–214.

that represent how aggressively policymakers adjust the Federal Funds Rate in response to deviations of GDP from trend and deviations of inflation from its target rate. Since the FOMC doesn't actually follow a stated rule, the parameters θ_1 and θ_2 have never been announced or even referenced by the FOMC in a policy statement.

We can use data to estimate what these parameters implicitly have been while Greenspan was chairman of the FOMC (and assuming that Bernanke is similar to Greenspan). As a first step, we rearrange the terms of equation (6.1) to

$$r_t^{ff} = \left[(1 - \theta_2)\, \pi^* + \bar{r}^{ff}\right] + \theta_1 \left[100.0 * \ln\left(GDP_t/GDP_t^*\right)\right]$$
$$+ \theta_2 \pi_t$$
$$= \theta_0 + \theta_1 \left[100.0 * \ln\left(GDP_t/GDP_t^*\right)\right] + \theta_2 \pi_t. \quad (6.2)$$

We then uncover θ_0, θ_1 and θ_2 by running a multivariate regression of the Federal Funds Rate on (a) a constant, (b) 100 times the deviation of $\ln(GDP_t)$ from its trend, and (c) the inflation rate. The regression uncovers the estimates for θ_0, θ_1, and θ_2 that best fit the available data. Note that θ_0, the constant in this regression, is equal to $(1 - \theta_2)\,\pi^* + \bar{r}^{ff}$. It is a constant as long as θ_2, π^*, and $\bar{r}^{ff}$ do not change over time. Obviously, the assumption of constancy is exactly that – an assumption – since the FOMC has never announced, or even explicitly mentioned, θ_2, π^*, or $\bar{r}^{ff}$.[7]

Before discussing the regression estimates, we should mention where the data can be found. Data on consumer price inflation

[7] Various members of the FOMC have hinted at preferred ranges of values for an inflation target π^*, but not all FOMC members agree on the appropriate range. See, for example, the speech by James Bullard, President of the Federal Reserve Bank of St. Louis, "Remarks on the US Economy and the State of the Housing Sector," made at the Wisconsin School of Business on June 6, 2008. The text of the speech is available at www.stlouisfed.org/news/speeches/2008/06_06_08.html.

(excluding food and energy) is available in NIPA Table 2.3.4; data on real GDP is available in NIPA Table 1.1.6; and data for the nominal effective Federal Funds Rate is available at the Federal Reserve's website.[8] I compute the log of potential GDP, $\ln(GDP^*)$, by regressing actual log real GDP on a constant and a time trend over the 1973:1–2007:4 period. The fitted value from this regression is set to equal the log of potential real GDP.[9]

After running the regression specified in equation (6.2) over the 1987:1–2007:4 sample period, I uncover the following coefficient estimates:

θ_0	θ_1	θ_2
1.840	0.616	1.161

The predicted value of the Federal Funds Rate that arises from this regression is shown as the dotted line in Figure 6.1. Obviously, the fit is not exact. The estimated Taylor rule underestimates the Federal Funds Rate by about two percentage points from 1994 to 1997, overestimates the Federal Funds Rate by about two percentage points from 2002 to 2005, and underestimates the Federal Funds Rate by about one percentage point from 2006 through year-end 2007.

Although the estimated Taylor rule does not fit the data perfectly, the coefficient estimates are useful because they show us, approximately, how the FOMC has historically adjusted the Federal Funds Rate in response to output and inflation. When real GDP is above trend, the Taylor rule estimate of $\theta_1 = 0.616$ suggests that policy makers set the Federal Funds Rate above its average level. And for

[8] See www.federalreserve.gov/releases/h15/data/Monthly/H15_FF_O.txt.
[9] A similar trend is uncovered by applying the HP-Filter with smoothing parameter $\lambda = 1,600$ to quarterly log real GDP over the 1973:1–2007:4 period. For more information on the HP-Filter, see Chapter 5.

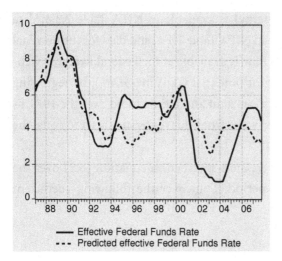

Figure 6.1 Nominal Federal Funds Rate and predicted Nominal Federal Funds Rate using equation (6.2), 1987:1–2007:4

each percentage point that inflation is above its target level, on average the Federal Funds Rate has increased by $\theta_2 = 1.161$ percentage points.

Note that even though the Federal Reserve only sets one interest rate, and it is the interest rate at which banks borrow reserves from each other, this interest rate is fundamentally linked to many (but not all) interest rates in the economy. These interest rates move together to limit opportunities for profits. For example, the interest rate for many shorter-duration Treasury Bills typically moves in tandem with changes to the Federal Funds Rate. If these other short-term interest rates do not move in tandem with the Federal Funds Rate, then banks can make profits (on a risk-adjusted basis) by borrowing (loaning) their reserves at the Federal Funds Rate and purchasing (selling) short-duration Treasuries whose yields do not adjust. In contrast, some interest rates in the economy should not be expected to change in response to changes in the Federal Funds Rate. For example, in an environment with a low and stable inflation rate, the yield on a 10-year Treasury should not be expected to respond much to temporary changes in the Federal Funds Rate. The reason is that the yield on a 10-year Treasury should reflect the entire path of short-term interest rates over the next 10 years, and temporary changes to the Federal Funds Rate are likely to net out over time.

6.3 Monetary Policy and Inflation

You might wonder why the Federal Reserve increases (decreases) the Federal Funds Rate whenever the rate of inflation is above (below) its target level.

Consider a situation in which the rate of inflation falls suddenly to a point where it is below its target level. If this happens, the Taylor rule suggests that the Federal Reserve will reduce the Federal Funds Rate in response. To implement a reduction in the Federal Funds Rate – the rate at which banks can borrow reserves overnight – the Federal Reserve buys Treasury Bills from banks and increases bank holdings of reserves in exchange. Banks can lend out excess reserves, so any increase in reserves also increases the quantity of loanable funds in the economy. Loanable funds are quickly convertible to cash or demand deposits. Thus, by increasing reserves, the Federal Reserve increases the potential supply of money. And, historically, changes to the supply of money have been positively correlated with changes to the overall price level, such that an increase in the supply of money should lead to an increase in the price level.

To understand the link between the supply of money and the price level, consider the following identity:

$$MV = PY. \tag{6.3}$$

In this equation, M is the stock of money and PY is nominal GDP, with P the price level and Y real GDP. V, called "velocity," describes how frequently money changes hands if all of nominal GDP is purchased using cash. For example, if nominal GDP is \$100 and the aggregate stock of money is \$50, then $V = 2$.

After taking logs, (6.3) becomes

$$\ln(M) + \ln(V) = \ln(P) + \ln(Y). \tag{6.4}$$

Now first difference to get

$$\Delta \ln(M) + \Delta \ln(V) = \Delta \ln(P) + \Delta \ln(Y). \tag{6.5}$$

Since $\Delta \ln(X) \approx \Delta X / X$ for any generic variable X,[10] this equation transforms to

$$\frac{\Delta M}{M} + \frac{\Delta V}{V} = \frac{\Delta P}{P} + \frac{\Delta Y}{Y} \tag{6.6}$$

$$\rightarrow \frac{\Delta V}{V} = \frac{\Delta P}{P} + \frac{\Delta Y}{Y} - \frac{\Delta M}{M} \tag{6.7}$$

$$\rightarrow g_V = g_P + g_Y - g_M. \tag{6.8}$$

where g_V, g_P, g_Y, and g_M stand for the growth rates of velocity, prices, real output, and money, respectively.

If velocity is approximately constant, such that $\Delta V / V \approx 0$, equation (6.8) implies that

$$g_M - g_Y \approx g_P. \tag{6.9}$$

Equation (6.9) suggests that, holding real output and velocity fixed, growth in the supply of money should directly translate to growth in the price level, inflation. The framework of this section is commonly

[10] $\Delta \ln(X) = \ln(X_{t+1}) - \ln(X_t)$ is equal to $\ln(X_{t+1}/X_t)$ which equals $\ln\left(1 + \frac{X_{t+1}-X_t}{X_t}\right)$. Since $\ln(1+z) \approx z$ when z is small, $\Delta \ln(X) \approx \frac{X_{t+1}-X_t}{X_t}$. See the appendix for details.

called the "quantity theory of money" and is attributable to Milton Friedman.[11]

To test this theory, we need to take a stand on what exactly "money" is. Three definitions of the stock of money are commonly used, M0, M1, and M2. These are defined as follows:

- M0 is the stock of currency plus reserves held by banks in their accounts with the Federal Reserve. M0 is sometimes called the "monetary base."
- M1 is currency in circulation, demand and other checkable deposits, and traveler's checks. This is typically what people think of as "money."
- M2 is equal to M1 plus close substitutes: retail money market mutual fund, savings, and (small) time deposits.

In Figure 6.2, I plot the quarterly time series of trend $g_M - g_Y$ against trend g_P, all at annual rates, over the 1959:1–2007:4 period. The trends are computed using the HP-Filter with smoothing parameter $\lambda = 1,600$. For g_Y I use the growth rate of real GDP; for g_P I use the growth rate of the GDP price index, where the GDP price index is defined as nominal GDP divided by real GDP; and for g_M I use the growth rate of the real stock of M2. The same graph with M1 does not show nearly the same tight pattern.[12] Data on nominal and real GDP are taken from Tables 1.1.5 and 1.1.6 of the NIPA. Data on M2 is taken from the H.6 release of the Federal Reserve Board, available at www.federalreserve.gov/releases/h6. The figure shows that there is a

[11] See M. Friedman, 1987, "Quantity Theory of Money," in *The New Palgrave Dictionary of Economics*, vol. IV, pp. 3–20, London: Palgrave.

[12] M2 growth has historically increased by about 1.3 percentage points per year faster than M1 growth. The same graph for M1 has the same qualitative patterns if 1.3 percent (annual rate) is added to $g_M - g_Y$.

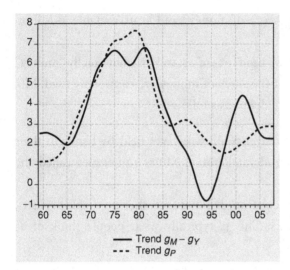

Figure 6.2 Trend $g_M - g_Y$ and trend g_P, annual rates, 1959:1–2007:4

very tight relationship between $g_M - g_Y$ and g_P until 1985. The correlation of the series between 1959:1 and 1984:4 is 0.94. After 1985, the relationship between $g_M - g_Y$ and g_P is much less pronounced, and the correlation of the series is only 0.07.

This does not mean that after 1985 there is no longer a link between money growth and inflation – rather, after 1985, M2 may not be the relevant definition of money and the GDP deflater may not be the appropriate price level. For comparison, Figure 6.3 plots the trend growth rate of M1 and trend growth in the consumer price index (from NIPA Table 2.3.4), annual rates, over the 1959:1–2007:4 period. In both cases, the trends are computed using the HP-Filter with $\lambda = 1,600$. After 1985, the correlation of these two series is 85 percent. Taken together, Figures 6.2 and 6.3 suggest that money growth and inflation are linked over time, but the exact relationship may have changed over time, and appears to be sensitive to the definitions of the price level and stock of money.

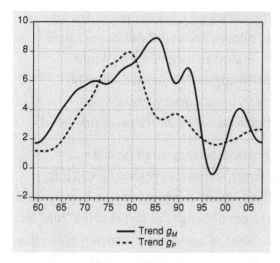

Figure 6.3 Trend g_M and trend g_P, annual rates, 1959:1–2007:4

FURTHER READING

- In the fall of 2008, as a response to the "credit crisis," the Federal
  Reserve no longer exclusively swapped Treasuries for reserves in its
  conduct of monetary policy. As of early 2009, the Federal Reserve
  has significant holdings of non-Treasury assets on its balance sheet.
  The actions and methods of the Federal Reserve during this crisis
  are still being debated, and as of the writing of this book it is too
  early to know the consequences of the actions. For a snapshot of the
  Fed's balance sheet and how it has changed, see the discussion at the
  Econbrowser blog from December 21, 2008, available at:
  www.econbrowser.com/archives/2008/12/federal_reserve_1.html.

- There is an ongoing debate amongst economists as to the value
  of discretion. That is, some macroeconomists have argued that
  macroeconomic performance would be improved if the FOMC

were to drop its discretion in setting monetary policy. For further reading about the "rules vs. discretion" debate, see J. Buol and M. Vaughan, 2003, "Rules vs. Discretion: The Wrong Choice Could Open the Floodgates," Regional Economist, Federal Reserve Bank of St. Louis, January, available at: http://stlouisfed.org/publications/ re/2003/a/pages/rules.html.

• Recently, the Bank of England has adopted an explicit and announced "inflation target," currently 2 percent for CPI inflation. The Bank of England adjusts its interest rate for the purpose of achieving its inflation target. Although this isn't exactly a "rule" for monetary policy, it provides less flexibility for monetary policy than in the US Federal Reserve System. A brief history and explanation of the Bank of England's inflation target is available in a document titled "Monetary Policy Framework" at the Bank of England website, www.bankofengland.co.uk/monetarypolicy/framework.htm.

• Due to the link between the supply of money and the price level, the two objectives of the Federal Reserve are sometimes at odds. As shown by the Taylor rule, in order to achieve the first mandate of "maximum employment," typically the Federal Reserve reduces the target Federal Funds Rate whenever GDP is below trend.[13] Historically, increases in bank reserves that have led to increases in the stock of money have also led to an increase in the price level. Thus, there may be circumstances where the first mandate of "maximum

---

[13] As an aside, this reduction in interest rates is consistent with the idea that all interest rates should be relatively low when the marginal product of capital is relatively low, which tends to occur when GDP is below trend. For example, if real GDP is produced according to $Y_t = z_t K_t^\alpha L_t^{1-\alpha}$, then, holding capital K_t and labor L_t fixed, a temporary downward shock to z_t will (a) reduce Y_t temporarily, and (b) reduce the marginal product of capital r_t temporarily since r_t is equal to $r_t = \alpha \frac{Y_t}{K_t}$. See Chapters 2 and 5 for details.

employment" may be at odds with the second mandate of the Federal Reserve, "stable prices."

H Homework

1 Download quarterly real GDP from Table 1.1.6 of the NIPA over the 1973:1 to 2007:4 period. Calculate trend log real GDP by regressing the natural logarithm of real GDP $\ln\left(GDP_t\right)$ against a constant and a time trend over the 1973:1–2007:4 period.[14] Assume the fitted value of this regression is exactly equal to trend log real GDP, i.e. $\ln\left(GDP_t^*\right)$.

Next, go to NIPA Table 2.3.4, "Price Indexes for Personal Consumption Expenditures by Major Type of Product," and download the quarterly data for line 25, "Personal consumption expenditures excluding food and energy," over the 1972:1–2007:4 period. Starting in 1973:1, compute the yearly percentage change to this index in each quarter. Denote the yearly percentage change as π_t.

Then, go to the H.15 release of the Federal Reserve Board and download the monthly effective federal funds rate (stated at an annual rate). Using the months appropriate for each quarter, compute the quarterly effective federal funds rate over the 1973:1–2007:4 period as the average value of the reported monthly rates.

Finally, use Microsoft Office Excel (or any statistical package) to regress over the 1973:1–1977:4 period the effective Federal Funds Rate (stated at an annual rate) on a constant and two variables: (1) the GDP gap, $100 * \left[\ln\left(GDP_t\right) - \ln\left(GDP_t^*\right)\right]$, and (2) the

---

[14] A time trend is a variable that increments by 1 in each period, i.e. is 1 in 1973:1, 2 in 1973:2, 3 in 1973:3, and so forth.

yearly percentage change to the personal consumption expenditures price index (line 35 of NIPA Table 2.3.4), π_t.[15] What regression coefficients do you estimate, and how do you interpret these estimates?

[15] Arthur Burns was the chairman of the Federal Reserve Board during this period.

Appendix: Math

O Objectives of this Appendix

In this appendix, I introduce you to a set of mathematical formulas that are essential for understanding many of the derivations in this book.

A.1 Derivatives

To start, you should know what a derivative is. A derivative describes the instantaneous rate of change of a function. Suppose there is some function out there $y = f(x)$. The derivative of y with respect to x tells you, approximately, how much y will change if x were to change by one unit.

Often times, a derivative is visualized as a tangent line on a function. See Figure A.1, where we have graphed a function and its derivative at two different points: at each point, the slope of the tangent line is the derivative.

Why does this matter? Well, when the function $y = f(x)$ is hump-shaped (such as the function in Figure A.1), the maximum value of the function is obtained at exactly the point where the derivative of that function equals zero.[1] Refer again to to Figure A.1. At exactly the point when the tangent to that function is flat – that is, the slope of the tangent line is zero – the function has achieved its maximum.

To make this point more concrete, suppose that $y = -5(x-3)^2$; this is the function that is graphed in Figure A.1. This function is hump-shaped, and is everywhere negative except at the point $x = 3$,

---

[1] When a function is bowl-shaped or U-shaped, the function minimum is obtained when the derivative is zero. Except for the case of the HP-Filter, discussed in Chapter 5, we will exclusively work with hump-shaped functions in this book.

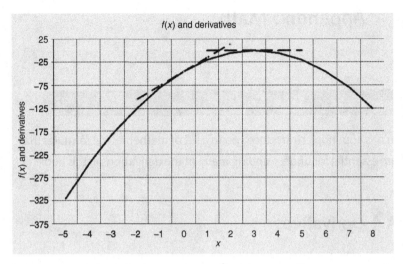

Figure A.1 Graph of $f(x) = -5(x-3)^2$, with tangent lines at $x = 0$ and $x = 3$

where it is equal to zero. So, at $x = 3$ the maximum value of the function is obtained. Now, suppose I were to tell you that the derivative of y with respect to x is $-10(x-3)$. This derivative is equal to zero at the point $x = 3$, the point at which the function maximum is achieved.

The derivative of a constant function, such as $y = 3$, is always zero. The derivative describes the rate of change of the function, and since a constant never changes value, the rate of change of a constant function is zero.

A.1.1 Derivative of Polynomials

You will need to know the formula for the derivatives of two different functions. First, you will need to be able to take the derivative of this function:

$$y = ax^n. \tag{A.1}$$

The derivative of y with respect to a, holding x constant (and thus holding x^n constant) is

$$\frac{\partial y}{\partial a} = x^n$$

where $\partial y / \partial a$ literally denotes "the derivative of y with respect to a." The derivative of y with respect to x, holding a constant, is

$$\frac{\partial y}{\partial x} = nax^{n-1}.$$

Take the special case of $n = 1$. Then the function in equation (A.1) is simply $y = ax$. The derivative of y with respect to a is equal to x, and the derivative of y with respect to x is equal to a. This special case will show up in our budget constraints for households and our cost function for firms.

But the function in (A.1) is also important to us because it turns out that a good approximation to a production function – a function that expresses output (Y) as a function of labor (L), capital (K), and technology (z) inputs – is the following:

$$Y = zK^{\alpha} L^{1-\alpha}. \tag{A.2}$$

This is called a Cobb–Douglas production function. We will repeatedly refer to this function throughout the book. Don't be scared by the Greek letter, α. α in equation (A.2) is serving the same role as n in equation (A.1). The derivative of Y in equation (A.2) with respect to K and only K (holding both z and L constant and thus $zL^{1-\alpha}$ constant) is

$$\frac{\partial Y}{\partial K} = \alpha \left[zL^{1-\alpha} \right] K^{\alpha-1}.$$

(I've grouped the variables that don't change together and placed them in the brackets so you would be less likely to be confused.) Similarly, the derivative of Y in equation (A.2) with respect to L and

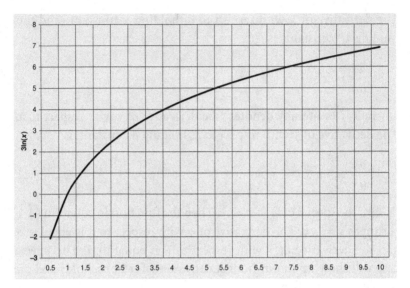

Figure A.2 Graph of $3 \ln (x)$

only L (holding z and K constant and thus zK^{α} constant) is

$$\frac{\partial Y}{\partial L} = (1 - \alpha) [zK^{\alpha}] L^{-\alpha}.$$

A.1.2 Derivative of the Natural Logarithm Function

There is a mathematical function called the "natural logarithm" that you may remember from your college calculus classes:

$$y = a \ln(x),$$

where ln means the natural logarithm. This function is plotted in Figure A.2 for a equal to 3.

In this case, the derivative of y with respect to x, holding a constant, is

$$\frac{\partial y}{\partial x} = \frac{a}{x}.$$

This is the amount that $\ln(x)$ would change, approximately, if x were to increase by 1 unit. If x were to increase by Δx units (instead of 1 unit), then $\ln(x)$ would approximately change by Δx times (a/x) units. Let's rearrange terms a little bit and use slightly different mathematical notation:

$$\frac{\Delta y}{\Delta x} = a \frac{\Delta x}{x}. \tag{A.3}$$

Note that $\Delta x/x$ is equal to the percentage change in x. This means the following: suppose that $a = 3$ and we want to know how much y will increase if x were to increase by 2 percent, so $\Delta x/x = 0.02$. Equation (A.3) tells us that y will change by 6 percent ($3 * 0.02 = 0.06$). Notice: y changes by 6 percent when x changes by 2 percent regardless of the initial values of x or y! The fact that the derivative of the natural logarithm function is related to the percentage change in x will be very useful throughout this book.

The natural logarithm function is also important to economists because we sometimes set household utility equal to the natural logarithm function. In other words, calling u utility and c consumption, economists often assume that $u = \ln(c)$. We use this utility function in many applications in this book.

The ln function has a few other features of which you should be aware:

- $\ln(1) = 0$.
- $\ln(a) + \ln(b) = \ln(ab)$
  $\ln(a) - \ln(b) = \ln(a/b)$.
- $\ln\left(a^b\right) = b\ln(a)$.

A.1.3 Derivative Approximation to the Natural Logarithm Function

As we noted before, the derivative of a function $y = f(x)$ measures approximately by how many units y would change if x were to increase by 1 unit. If x were to increase by z units, then the function y would approximately change by z times the derivative.

A general rule for any function, then, is that:

$$y = f(x + z)$$
$$\approx f(x) + z\frac{\partial y}{\partial x},$$

where the function derivative $\partial y / \partial x$ is evaluated at x. This is called a first-order Taylor series expansion. The smaller in magnitude z is, the more accurate the approximation.

Now, let's apply this to the natural log function:

$$y = \ln(x + z)$$
$$\approx \ln(x) + z\frac{1}{x},$$

where in this case $1/x$ is the derivative of $\ln(x)$ with respect to x. This is a really useful approximation when $x = 1$ and z is a small number. Then, we have

$$y = \ln(1 + z)$$
$$\approx z.$$

We get this result because $\ln(1) = 0$.

A.2 Constrained Optimization: Econ 1 Revealed

In this section, I am going to teach you the tools of constrained optimization. This will involve a concept called a Lagrange multiplier.

Suppose that households get utility from two consumption goods: apples a and bananas b. Define household utility from apples and bananas as

$$u = \phi \ln(a) + (1 - \phi) \ln(b).$$

All ϕ does in the above equation is relate preferences for apples to bananas. For example, if ϕ were a number near 1.0, then many bananas would be needed to compensate households for the loss of one apple. Alternatively, if ϕ were a number near 0, then very few bananas would be needed to compensate households for the loss of one apple. Also note that we are only considering cases of ϕ between 0 and 1; it turns out that this is not a restriction at all on preferences[2] and further, setting ϕ between 0 and 1 makes the linkages of "expenditure shares" and real GDP growth immediate, as discussed in Chapter 1 of the book.

Suppose the goal of a household is to maximize its utility from apples and bananas subject to not spending more than its income. Denoting the price of apples as p_a and the price of bananas as p_b, the "budget constraint" of households is

$$I - p_a a - p_b b \geq 0,$$

where I denotes income.[3]

Now what you've probably done in your introductory microeconomics classes is draw a line representing the budget constraint, drawn an indifference curve mapping the tradeoff of apples to bananas required to keep utility fixed at some level, found the point where the indifference curve is tangent to the budget constraint, and talked your way through why this tangent point represented the utility-maximizing combination of apples and bananas.

A.2.1 Writing Down and Solving the Problem

Have you ever wondered what the math was behind those Econ 1 graphs? Here we go. You are about to see a mechanical technique to

[2] We will show that what matters is the ratio $\phi/(1-\phi)$; we can always define a ϕ such that this ratio is equal to any given positive number.
[3] For technical reasons, it is important that we write the budget constraint as income less expenditures. The reason that we have a $\geq$ sign (and not an $=$ sign) is less important.

solve "constrained optimization" problems. It is nothing more than a technique. Memorize how to do it.

Households have two choices: (1) the number of apples and (2) the number of bananas to purchase. They also have one constraint: the budget constraint. The way to solve this constrained optimization problem is to write down the following function:

$$[\phi \ln(a) + (1 - \phi) \ln(b)] + \lambda (I - p_a a - p_b b). \qquad (A.4)$$

The piece in the square brackets in (A.4) is household utility. The second piece – the piece multiplied by the Greek letter λ – is the budget constraint. Mathematicians call λ a Lagrange multiplier. Thus, the function we have written down is the the utility function plus λ times the budget constraint.

To find the utility-maximizing quantity of applies and bananas subject to the budget constraint being satisfied, take the derivative of equation (A.4) twice – once with respect to the choice of apples (a) and a second time with respect to the choice of bananas (b). In each case, set the derivative equal to zero, which, as we stated earlier, is a condition for function maximization.

Using our tools from the previous pages, we can easily set the derivative of (A.4) with respect to apples to zero:

$$\frac{\phi}{a} - \lambda p_a = 0. \qquad (A.5)$$

Remember that when we take the derivative with respect to apples, we only worry about taking the derivative of terms that have apples term a in them. Any term that does not have an a in it is being held constant, and, as we noted, the derivative of a constant is zero.

Setting the derivative of (A.4) with respect to bananas to zero (holding apples constant) is equally easy:

$$\frac{1 - \phi}{b} - \lambda p_b = 0. \qquad (A.6)$$

Solve out for λ and you get our condition for optimality:

$$\frac{\frac{\phi}{a}}{\frac{1-\phi}{b}} = \frac{p_a}{p_b}.$$

In words: when households optimally purchase apples and bananas, the ratio of the marginal utility of apples to the marginal utility of bananas (the left-hand side) is equal to the ratio of prices (the right-hand side). This is the mathematics behind your Econ 1 graphs.

A.2.2 Notes on the Lagrange Multiplier (λ) and Expenditure Shares

Although we have solved for the optimality condition, we have not explicitly solved for the amount of apples and bananas that the household purchases.

To do this, we first solve for λ. With terms rearranged, equation (A.5) states $\lambda p_a a = \phi$. Similarly, equation (A.6) states $\lambda p_b b = 1 - \phi$. Add these two together to get $\lambda (p_a a + p_b b) = \phi + 1 - \phi = 1$. Now use the relationship that $I = p_a a + p_b b$. This gives us the following expression:

$$\lambda = \frac{1}{I}. \tag{A.7}$$

λ is therefore linked to income. If income were to increase, λ would fall.

Now substitute equation (A.7) back into equations (A.5) and (A.6). After rearranging some terms, this yields

$$a p_a = \phi I$$

$$b p_b = (1 - \phi) I.$$

What have we learned? $a p_a$ is total expenditures on apples and $b p_b$ is total expenditures on bananas. The expenditure share on apples is $a p_a / I$ and the expenditure share on bananas is $b p_b / I$. Thus, with the assumption on utility we have made, optimal expenditure shares are constant and independent of prices. When expenditure shares are constant, as they are in this example, p_a and p_b can be any positive number, and households will always spend ϕ fraction of their income on apple purchases and $1 - \phi$ fraction of their income on banana purchases.

Bibliography

Andolfatto, D., 1996, "Business Cycles and Labor-Market Search," *American Economic Review*, vol. 86, pp. 112–132.

Bailey, R., 2001, "Post-Scarcity Prophet: Economist Paul Romer on Growth, Technological Change, and an Unlimited Human Future," *Reason* magazine, December. Available at www.reason.com/news/show/ 28243.html.

Bansal, R. and A. Yaron, 2004, "Risks for the Long Run: A Potential Resolution of Asset Pricing Puzzles," *Journal of Finance*, vol. 59, pp. 1481–1509.

Bernanke, B., 2004, "Remarks by Governor Ben S. Bernanke at the Meetings of the Eastern Economic Association on the Great Moderation, Washington DC," Federal Reserve Board of Governors. Available at www.federalreserve.gov/boarddocs/speeches/2004/20040220/default. htm.

Boarini, R., A. Johansson, and M. Mira d'Ercole, 2006, "Alternative Measures of Well Being," OECD Social, Employment and Migration Working Papers No. 33. Available at www.oecd.org/dataoecd/13/38/ 36165332.pdf.

Bullard, J., 2008, "Remarks on the US Economy and the State of the Housing Sector," made at the Wisconsin School of Business, June 6, 2008. Available at www.stlouisfed.org/news/speeches/ 2008/06_06_08.html.

Buol, J. and M. Vaughan, 2003, "Rules vs. Discretion: The Wrong Choice Could Open the Floodgates," Regional Economist, Federal Reserve Bank of St. Louis, January. Available at http://stlouisfed.org/ publications/re/2003/a/pages/rules.html.

Bureau of Economic Analysis Website, 2003, "Fixed Assets and Consumer Durable Goods in the United States, 1925–97," September. Available at www.bea.gov/national/pdf/Fixed_Assets_1925_97.pdf.

2006, "A Guide to the National Income and Product Accounts of the United States," September. Available at www.bea.gov/methodologies/index.htm.

Campbell, J. Y. and R. J. Shiller, 1988, "The Dividend-Price Ratio and Expectations of Future Dividends and Discount Factors," *Review of Financial Studies*, vol. 1, pp. 195–228.

Campbell, S., M. Davis, J. Gallin, and R. Martin, 2008, "What Moves Housing Markets: A Variance Decomposition of the Rent-Price Ratio," Working Paper, University of Wisconsin-Madison.

Cecchetti, S., A. Flores-Lagunes, and S. Krause, 2006, "Assessing the Sources of Changes in the Volatility of Real Growth," National Bureau of Economic Research Working Paper 11946, Cambridge, MA.

Cochrane, J., 2001, *Asset Pricing*. Princeton, NJ: Princeton University Press.

Cobb, C. W. and P. H. Douglas, 1928, "A Theory of Production," *American Economic Review*, vol. 8, pp. 139–165.

Cooley, T. and E. Prescott, 1995, "Economic Growth and Business Cycles," in *Frontiers of Business Cycle Research*, edited by Thomas F. Cooley. Princeton, NJ: Princeton University Press.

Davis, M. A. and J. Heathcote, 2005, "Housing and the Business Cycle," *International Economic Review*, vol. 46, pp. 751–784.

Davis, M. A. and J. Heathcote, 2007, "The Price and Quantity of Residential Land in the United States," *Journal of Monetary Economics*, vol. 54, pp. 2595–2620.

Davis, M. A., A. Lehnert, and R. F. Martin, 2008, "The Rent-Price Ratio for the Aggregate Stock of Owner-Occupied Housing," *Review of Income and Wealth*, vol. 54, pp. 279–284.

Davis, M. A. and R. F. Martin, 2009, "Housing, Home Production, and the Equity and Value Premium Puzzles," *Journal of Housing Economics*, forthcoming.

Federal Reserve Bank of St. Louis Website, "In Plain English: Making Sense of the Federal Reserve." Available at www.stls.frb.org/publications/pleng/PDF/PlainEnglish.pdf.

Fraumeini, B., 1997, "The Measurement of Depreciation in the U.S. National Income and Product Accounts," Survey of Current Business, July. Available at www.bea.gov/scb/pdf/national/niparel/ 1997/0797fr.pdf.

Friedman, M., 1987, "Quantity Theory of Money," in *The New Palgrave Dictionary of Economics*, vol. IV, pp. 3–20. London and New York: Palgrave and Stockton.

Gomme, P. and P. Rupert, 2007, "Theory, Measurement and Calibration of Macroeconomic Models," *Journal of Monetary Economics*, vol. 54, pp. 460–497.

Green, R. K. and S. Malpezzi, 2003, *A Primer on U.S. Housing Markets and Housing Policy.* Washington, DC: Urban Institute Press, for the American Real Estate and Urban Economics Association.

Hagedorn, M. and I. Manovskii, 2008, "The Cyclical Behavior of Equilibrium Unemployment and Vacancies Revisited," *American Economic Review*, vol. 98, pp. 1692–1706.

Heston, A., R. Summers, and B. Aten, 2006, Penn World Table Version 6.2, Center for International Comparisons of Production, Income and Prices at the University of Pennsylvania, September. Available at http://pwt.econ.upenn.edu/php_site/pwt_index.php.

Hodrick, R. and E. Prescott, 1997, "Postwar U.S. Business Cycles: An Empirical Investigation," *Journal of Money, Credit, and Banking*, vol. 29, pp. 1–16.

Kim, C. and C. Nelson, 1999, "Has the US Economy Become More Stable? A Bayesian Approach Based on a Markov-Switching Model of the Business Cycle," *Review of Economics and Statistics*, vol. 81, pp. 608–616.

Kydland, F. and E. Prescott, 1982, "Time to Build and Aggregate Fluctuations," *Econometrica*, vol. 50, pp. 1345–1370.

Lucas, R. E., Jr., 1981, *Studies in Business Cycle Theory.* Cambridge, MA: MIT Press.

Lucas, R. and L. Rapping, 1969, "Real Wages, Employment, and Inflation," *Journal of Political Economy*, vol. 77, pp. 721–754.

Mehra, R. and E. Prescott, 1985, "The Equity Premium: A Puzzle," *Journal of Monetary Economics*, vol. 15, pp. 145–161.

Mendoza, E., A. Razin, and L. Tesar, 1994, "Effective Tax Rates in Macroeconomics. Cross-country Estimates of Tax Rates on Factor Income and Consumption," *Journal of Monetary Economics*, vol. 34, pp. 297–323.

The MELON project website, 2009, "MacroEconomics Laboratory ONline." Available at http://melon.uib.no/projects/melon.

Mishkin, F. S., 2007, "Monetary Policy and the Dual Mandate," speech at Bridgewater College, Bridgewater, Virginia, April 10, 2007,

Federal Reserve Board of Governors. Text of speech available at www.
federalreserve.gov/newsevents/speech/mishkin20070410a.htm.

Parente, S., R. Rogerson, and R. Wright, 2000, "Homework in Development
Economics: Household Production and the Wealth of Nations," *Journal
of Political Economy*, vol. 108, pp. 680–687.

Pesendorfer, W., 2006, "Behavioral Economics Comes of Age: A Review
Essay on Advances in Behavioral Economics," *Journal of Economic
Literature*, vol. 44, pp. 712–721.

Ramey, V. and N. Francis, 2009, "A Century of Work and Leisure," *American
Economic Journal: Macroeconomics*, forthcoming.

Shimer, R., 2005, "The Cyclical Behavior of Equilibrium Unemployment
and Vacancies," *American Economic Review*, vol. 95, pp. 25–49.

Social Security Administration Website, 1996, "Toward a More Accurate
Measure of the Cost of Living. Final Report to the Senate Finance Com-
mittee from the Advisory Commission to Study the Consumer Price
Index." Available at www.ssa.gov/history/reports/boskinrpt.html.

Taylor, J., 1993, "Discretion Versus Policy Rules in Practice," *Carnegie-
Rochester Series on Public Policy*, vol. 39, pp. 195–214.

Index

agencies, bureaus, organizations
  Bureau of Economic Analysis or BEA, 8,
    11, 17, 23, 37, 69, 73, 101, 150
  Bureau of Labor Statistics or BLS, 32, 37,
    76, 115
  Federal Reserve or FOMC, 15, 192–205
  National Bureau of Economic Research or
    NBER, 169
  Organization for Economic Cooperation
    and Development or OECD, 37
autarky or closed economy, 144, 155,
  159

capital
  capital stock, 20, 26, 45, 53, 59, 66, 99, 130,
    133, 159, 211
  depreciation, 21, 49, 58, 68, 73, 83
Cobb–Douglas production, 46, 80, 159, 211
constraints
  budget constraint, 24, 93, 100, 157, 184,
    215
  time constraint, 93, 137

Decennial Census of Housing, 125
discount factor or discount rate, 92, 104, 122,
  130
dual mandate, 195
durable goods, 17, 33, 69, 135

expansion or boom, 92, 169, 186
expenditure share, 6, 8, 11, 32, 217

GDP
  base year, 5
  definition, 3
  expenditure method, 15
    consumption, 16
    government spending, 22

    investment, 20
    net exports, 25
  income method, 28
    consumption of fixed capital, 30
    corporate profits, 30
    net interest, 30
    proprietors' income, 30
    statistical discrepancy, 28, 30
  non-marketed production, 15
GNP, 9
government activities
  budget deficit, 24
  crowding out, 24
  educational spending, 23
  taxes, 23, 30, 64, 74
  transfer payments, 23, 30

housing rent or price, 17, 35, 118

income
  capital income, 28, 50, 65, 101
  disposable income, 24
  labor income, 28, 51, 93, 101, 133
inflation
  Boskin Commission, 37
  covered interest parity, 163
  definition, 31
  equipment and software prices, 35
  expectations, 128
  Fisher equation, 164
  food and energy prices, 33
  historical experience, 13, 33, 187
  hyperinflation, 38
  monetary policy, 197
  price controls, 13
  quantity theory of money, 202
interest rate or rate of return, 27, 49, 56, 64,
  99, 154, 159, 185, 197

labor, 16, 45, 51, 53, 59, 67, 76, 93, 101, 129,
159, 211
leisure, 78, 93, 130

marginal products, 47, 56, 74, 159,
185
mathematics and statistics
correlation, 181, 204
covariance, 112, 181
derivative, 11, 48, 94, 100, 177, 209
expected value, 106, 113
HP-Filter, 20, 175, 199, 203, 209
infinite sum, 122
L'Hôpital's rule, 103
Lagrange multiplier, 95, 100, 108, 111,
119, 131, 214, 217
logarithm, 10, 53, 80, 103, 169, 178, 199,
212
standard deviation, 20
Taylor series approximation, 12, 214
variance, 181
money, 36, 152, 192

national accounts
fixed asset tables, 69
flow of funds, 134

National Income and Product Accounts or
NIPA, 11, 17, 22, 24, 28, 32, 51, 70,
77, 80, 101, 150, 199, 203
Penn World Tables or PWT, 60, 61, 63,
84
SNA 93, 18

preferences, 9, 93, 104, 132, 215

recession or contraction, 80, 169

standard of living, 4, 9, 15, 146, 153

technology, 16, 45, 52, 57, 59, 72, 80, 154,
159, 186, 187, 211
trade deficit, 26, 149, 151
trend, cycle, fluctuations, 12, 18, 56, 72, 78,
82, 133, 171, 178, 184, 197, 203

utility or marginal utility, 4, 9, 16, 78, 93, 97,
102, 133, 153, 184, 213, 214, 217

velocity, 202

wealth, 26, 97, 101, 111
Wikipedia, 38, 84, 135, 163, 193